Cold Soups

Cold Soups

Nina Graybill and Maxine Rapoport

Farragut Publishing Company
Washington, D.C.
1988

PRINTED IN THE UNITED STATES OF AMERICA

Book design by Kevin Osborn, Research & Design Associates

Cover illustration by Judy Barczak

Second printing 1990

Library of Congress Cataloging-in-Publication Data

Graybill, Nina.
  Cold soups.

  1. Soups. 2. Cookery (Cold dishes) I. Rapoport,
Maxine. II. Title.
TX757.G7 1988   641.8'13   88-21286
ISBN 0-918535-07-7

To Steve and Phoebe with love,
N.G. and M.R.

Introduction

Cold soups are a delight — at once flavorful, refreshing and elegant. They are made to order for today's busy life styles. Their variety and flavors are almost endless; vichyssoise or jellied consomme may be the most familiar cold soups, but consider Tuscany White Bean Soup with Bacon and El Tamarindo Corn Soup for a change of pace. Moreover, cold soups based on fresh vegetables, and there are many in this book, are wonderfully nutritious.

Cold soups are ideal for entertaining: they can be made ahead of time (most several days ahead) and many of them freeze successfully. They begin a dinner party on a luxurious note, but can also stand as the centerpiece of a light lunch for guests. And they are ideal for family suppers, especially on steamy summer evenings when no one is in the mood to cook or to eat hot, heavy food.

But cold soups need not be limited to warm weather. A light cold soup can be a welcome if unexpected first course for a mid-winter meal. Then again, a number of the recipes in this book can be served hot; simply adjust the seasonings to suit your taste, keeping in mind that chilling lessens the intensity of herbs and spices and the cold soup recipes in this book take that factor into account.

Dieters and those on restricted diets need not despair. Reduce calories and lower cholesterol levels by omitting the cream and/or egg yolks. If the soup seems too thin, puree a boiled potato along with the soup.

We appreciate the many cold soup recipes passed along by family and friends. A special thanks to Nahum Waxman of Kitchen Arts & Letters in New York and Nancy Marcus of The Cookbook Stall in Philadelphia, each of whom encouraged us to write this book.

Nina Graybill and Maxine Rapoport

Contents

Tips About Cold Soup

Tips About Cold Soup

Over the many years we have served cold soups to family and friends, we've developed a number of tips about making and serving those delicious concoctions. This chapter shares them with you.

• Always taste the soup just before serving: correct seasonings, especially salt and pepper, to suit yourself.

• If you add salt to the simmering broth, start with 1/4 teaspoon or less. Stocks and broths — especially the canned variety — vary greatly in salt content. Add more salt to taste after soup is cold and flavors have blended.

• Once soup has chilled, thin if necessary to desired consistency by adding broth, cream or milk a few tablespoons at a time, mixing well after each addition.

• Reconstitute separated soups by whirling in the blender or food processor or by stirring with a wire whisk.

• For safety's sake, always cool soup before pureeing in the blender or food processor — and puree it in small batches. Heat causes the pureed mixture to expand and a sudden overflow of hot soup is not only extremely messy, it can cause serious burns.

• Whenever possible, let soup chill overnight or at least 4-6 hours. The result is a richer, deeper flavor. Cover bowl tightly with plastic wrap. For soups that change color when exposed to air — non-citrus fruits and avocado, for example — place plastic wrap directly on top of the soup, then cover bowl with a second piece of wrap.

- Most cold soups have more flavor if they're chilled, not icy cold. You might want to remove non-dessert soups from the refrigerator 1/2 hour before serving.

- Thoroughly wash all vegetables. Peel carrots, potatoes and the like unless otherwise indicated.

- Heavy cream means whipping cream. For light cream, use table cream, half and half or a mixture of milk and whipping cream.

- Use white pepper if you find black specks in pale soups unappealing; the flavor is the same.

- Pass around a variety of packaged crackers with the soup, or serve one of the more elaborate choices in the Accompaniments section of this book.

- Serve two or more cold soups in the same bowl, just as upscale restaurants do. Pick two, three or even four recipes that contrast in color but are complementary in flavor; thick cream soups work best. For example, a deep orange carrot soup, a bright green pea soup and a pale cauliflower soup not only taste good together but look pretty as well.

If you are using two soups, there are several approaches you might try: First, pour about 5 ounces of one soup into each serving bowl, then pour 1 or 2 ounces of the second soup in a pattern on top of the first (thinned sour cream may also be used). Another technique is to pour the second soup in a straight line across the first, then make perpendicular "cuts" through it with a table knife. Experiment — a different pattern in each bowl is especially attractive. You can also serve the soups side by side: Pour about 3 ounces of the soups into two measuring cups with spouts; hold the two cups over the bowl with spouts close together and pour evenly. If you have a helper and extra measuring cups, try three or four soups. Red, green and yellow pepper soups, each seasoned differently, look stunning in the same bowl.

• Serve in style: For a formal dinner, place soup bowls in larger containers of crushed ice. The once-fashionable Supreme glass bowls are wonderful for cold soups; scavenge your grandmother's or mother's china closet for a set. For a dinner party, a first course soup served in demitasse cups in the living room gets things off to a lively start. Crystal bowls, icy from the freezer, are a welcome sight on a hot day. Double old-fashioned glasses make great containers for soup drinks.

Have first course soups already on the table — or serve your guests from a crystal bowl using a silver ladle. Dust off those inherited two-handled cream soups or the pottery bowls you bought on vacation; consider using elaborate or oversized wineglasses. Conventional soup spoons may seem too large; use teaspoons, round soup spoons, even demitasse spoons. Small plates under each bowl provide a place to rest the spoon.

Accompaniments

Accompaniments

A little something to nibble along with a cold soup is always a nice touch. A basket of "store bought" crackers is one answer. Bakery breads are another. More interesting — and really very little extra work — are the accompaniments included in this chapter. All can be prepared ahead and baked or reheated at the last minute. Your selection should depend on how light or heavy your entree is. You might, for example, be serving a main-course salad; in that case, look for an accompaniment to the first course soup that is a little more substantial, such as the Garlic-Swiss French Bread, and serve it with the main course as well. For heavier main courses such as roasts and casseroles, pass Seasoned Pita Crisps with the first course cold soup.

Italian Toast

1 loaf best quality Italian bread, sliced into 3/4-inch thick slices
6 tablespoons olive oil
3 tablespoons red wine vinegar
2 cloves garlic, peeled and put through a garlic press
Salt and freshly ground black pepper to taste
1/2 teaspoon red pepper flakes

Place bread slices on a cookie sheet. Whisk together other ingredients, spread generously on the bread. About 10 minutes before serving, place in a 400-degree oven and bake until hot and crispy. Serve in a bread basket lined with a cloth napkin. May also be served at room temperature.

Serves 6.

Crostini

12 1/2-inch slices best quality Italian bread
12 scant teaspoons extra-virgin olive oil
12 1/4-inch slices whole milk mozzarella cheese to fit bread
1 can flat anchovies, drained and sliced lengthwise so that you have 24 slivers
12 pats of butter

Spread a teaspoon of oil on each bread slice. Place a slice of cheese on the bread, place two pieces of anchovy on the cheese in an "X" shape, and top all with a pat of butter. Place bread on a cookie sheet.

Bake in a preheated 375-degree oven until cheese is bubbly and bottom of bread is lightly browned, about 10 minutes.

Serves 6.

Casseri Toast

12 ounces imported casseri cheese
12 1/2-inch slices good French baguette (about 2 inches in diameter)
4 tablespoons olive oil
1 teaspoon dried leaf oregano

Slice the French bread rounds in half again crosswise, for a total of 24 pieces. Place on cookie sheet in 350-degree oven and bake about 10 to 15 minutes until bread has crisped. Remove.

Grate casseri and put in a heavy skillet; add olive oil and oregano. Melt over very low heat, stirring occasionally.

Dip one side of the bread in the cheese mixture, making sure each piece has oil and cheese on it.

If made ahead, may be reheated in a 350-degree oven about 10 minutes or until hot. Serve in a basket lined with a cloth napkin.

Serves 6.

Seasoned Pita Crisps

*W*edges *of pita bread, seasoned with herbs and spices and crisped in the oven, make tasty, not-too-filling accompaniments for cold soup. To prepare, blend topping ingredients, then spread on pita rounds. Cut each pita into quarters or sixths. Bake in a 400-degree oven until crisp and hot, about 5 minutes. Serve in a napkin-lined basket.*

6 small pitas, about 7 inches in diameter

Topping #1:
1/2 stick butter, softened, or 1/4 cup olive oil
1 bunch scallions, washed and finely minced including tops
Salt and freshly ground black pepper to taste

Topping #2:
1/2 stick butter, softened, or 1/4 cup olive oil
3 small cloves garlic, finely minced
1/2 cup grated Parmesan cheese
Salt to taste

Topping #3:
1/2 stick butter, softened, or 1/4 cup olive oil
3 small cloves garlic, finely minced
1/2 teaspoon red pepper flakes
Salt to taste

Topping #4:
1/2 stick butter, softened, or 1/4 cup olive oil
1 tablespoon dried dillweed
1/2 teaspoon red pepper flakes
Salt to taste

Cheese Croutons

1 loaf French or Italian bread
Approximately 1/2 cup olive oil
1 cup mild white cheese (such as Monterey jack or whole milk mozzarella), grated
Red pepper flakes (optional)
Salt to taste

Slice bread into 12 1/2-inch-thick pieces; if bread is large, slice each piece in half crosswise. Spread generously with olive oil. Bake in a 350-degree oven until lightly browned. Sprinkle with the grated cheese, salt, and the optional red pepper flakes. May be made ahead of time to this point and covered.

At serving time, reheat bread, uncovered, in a preheated 400-degree oven about 5 minutes, or until cheese is bubbly.

Serves 6.

Cheese Straws

1 package frozen puff pastry, thawed
1/2 cup grated Parmesan cheese
2-3 dashes ground red pepper
1/2 teaspoon ground cumin
1/2 teaspoon salt
1/4 teaspoon freshly grated black pepper

In a small bowl, mix together all but the puff pastry. Roll out the pastry into a 7- by 12-inch rectangle. Press the cheese mixture into both sides of the pastry. Cut pastry into 1/2-inch-wide ribbons. Using both hands, grasp the ends of each ribbon and twist in opposite directions to create a rippled effect. Place on a greased cookie sheet. Bake in a 400-degree oven until straws are puffed and lightly browned, about 12 minutes. Store in an airtight container.

Makes 24 straws.

Pumpernickel or Rye Croutons

1 unsliced loaf pumpernickel or rye with seeds
1 stick butter
1/2 teaspoon garlic powder
1/2 teaspoon salt
1/2 teaspoon mixed Italian seasonings

Preheat oven to 300 degrees. Cut bread, including crusts, into 1-inch cubes. Combine butter and seasonings and melt over low heat; do not let brown. In a large bowl, toss together the bread cubes and butter mixture until bread is well coated. Spread cubes on a cookie sheet and bake until firm and dry, about 45 minutes. Let cool and store in airtight container. To serve, float a few cubes on soup or pass in a basket.

Makes approximately 6 cups of croutons.

Herbed Pita Triangles

4 large loaves pita bread
1 stick butter, softened
2 tablespoons chopped parsley
1 tablespoon minced green onion
1 tablespoon lemon juice
1/2 teaspoon each, thyme and basil, crushed
1 large garlic clove, minced
1/4 teaspoon salt
Freshly ground pepper to taste

Separate each pita into two rounds; cut each round into sixths.

Put butter and remaining ingredients into processor or blender and beat until combined. Or place butter and all ingredients in a small bowl and mix thoroughly with a fork.

Spread inside of pita triangles with butter mixture, place on cookie sheet, cover and refrigerate or freeze until needed. Bake in 400-degree oven 5 minutes or until slightly crisp and brown.

Yields 48 pieces.

Garlic-Swiss French Bread

2 cups grated Swiss cheese
2 garlic cloves, minced
1/2 teaspoon thyme
1/4 cup white wine
2 tablespoons finely chopped parsley
1/2 loaf French bread

Mix all ingredients except bread together, set aside. Slice bread vertically, 1-inch thick, almost to bottom. Press cheese mixture between
each slice. Wrap bread in foil and refrigerate until 30 minutes before
serving. Bake bread, in foil, at 400-degrees for 20 minutes.

Yields 12-15 slices.

Anchovy-Caper Crisps

1 tin flat anchovy fillets
1 heaping tablespoon capers
1 tablespoon white wine vinegar
1/2 cup good quality olive oil
Freshly ground black pepper
12-15 1/2-inch slices of French bread or Italian bread sliced in half

In processor or blender puree anchovies, capers, vinegar and olive oil, or mash together with a fork. Spread mixture on top of bread slices. Sprinkle with freshly ground black pepper. Place slices on a cookie sheet and bake in 425-degree oven until toasted and bubbly. Serve hot.

Yields 12-15 slices.

Dan's Beer Biscuits

4 cups packaged biscuit mix
3 tablespoons sugar
1 can beer, just opened

Mix all ingredients in a bowl. Half-fill either greased or paper-lined muffin pans with the batter. Bake in preheated 350-degree oven about 20 minutes. Cool on rack. If not using right away, wrap with foil and freeze until needed. Reheat frozen muffins, wrapped in foil, in preheated 350 degree oven about 20 minutes.

Yields 16-18 muffins.

Double-Wheat Mini Biscuits

3/4 cup all-purpose flour
1/2 cup whole wheat flour
2 tablespoons wheat germ
1/2 teaspoon salt
1/4 cup soft butter (If using processor, butter must be hard)
1 teaspoon caraway seeds
1/2 cup milk, 1 tablespoon reserved

Combine flours, wheat germ and salt in a medium bowl or in processor. Cut in butter with fork or with on-off pulses of processor until crumbly. Blend in caraway seeds and milk.

Scrape out onto floured pastry cloth or other surface and shape into a 1/2-inch-thick circle. Fold two sides over center and roll out to 1/2-inch-thick circle. Cut with small (1-1/2 inch) biscuit cutter or top of small glass. Place on greased cookie sheet and bake in preheated 425-degree oven 15 to 20 minutes. Cool on rack, then store in cookie tin or place in heavy plastic bag and freeze until needed. Reheat frozen biscuit wrapped in foil in preheated 350-degree oven about 20 minutes.

Yields about 20 biscuits.

Cheddar-Chili Bread

1 16-ounce package hot roll or bread mix
2 cups grated sharp cheddar cheese
3 tablespoons chopped canned chilies, drained
1 egg, lightly beaten
1-2 tablespoons grated Parmesan cheese

Follow package directions for preparing bread, stir in cheese and chilies. After the 5-minute rest period, roll dough into a 1-inch thick rectangle, then roll up from the short end, jelly-roll fashion, and fit into greased 9 x 4-1/2-inch bread pan. Cover and let rise in warm place about 15 minutes. Brush with beaten egg and sprinkle with grated Parmesan cheese. Bake in preheated 375-degree oven about 30 minutes or until bread sounds hollow when tapped on top. Cool on rack. Serve warm.

May be frozen, wrapped in double foil after it is thoroughly cool, up to 1 month. Reheat wrapped in foil, in 350-degree oven, about 25 minutes.

Yields about 12 slices.

Quick and Snappy Parsley Bread

3 cups all-purpose flour
3/4 cup chopped parsley
1 teaspoon dried red pepper flakes
1-1/2 tablespoons baking powder
1/2 teaspoon seasoned salt
1 stick soft butter, or well chilled if using processor
1 cup light cream
1 tablespoon melted butter
Coarsely ground black pepper

Combine flour, parsley, pepper flakes, baking powder and salt in large
bowl or bowl of procesor fitted with steel blade. Mix together. Add
butter, cut in slices, and cut in with fork or pulse on and off until crumbly. Stir in cream with fork, or pour through feed tube, with machine
running, and blend just until incorporated. Turn dough out onto floured
pastry cloth or other floured surface. Shape into an 8 or 9-inch circle.
Transfer to greased cookie sheet, brush with melted butter and sprinkle
with coarsely ground black pepper. Bake in preheated 425-degree oven
about 25-30 minutes or until golden brown and bread sounds hollow
when tapped on top.

Yields 1 loaf.

Cheese Pepper Biscuits

3/4 cup Fontina cheese, grated fine
1 scant teaspoon dried red pepper flakes
2 cups all-purpose flour
2 teaspoons baking powder
1 teaspoon baking soda
1/2 teaspoon salt
4 tablespoons soft butter, or well-chilled if using food processor
1 cup buttermilk, or 1 cup milk mixed with 1 tablespoon vinegar or lemon juice
1 egg white, lightly beaten

Mix cheese, pepper flakes, and dry ingredients together in a large bowl. Cut in butter with pastry blender or fork. Add buttermilk and stir together with fork just until mixed. Turn out on to floured surface and knead 10-12 times. Roll out to a 1/2-inch-thick circle and cut with biscuit cutter, using either a small 1-1/2-inch cutter or the standard-size larger cutter. Place on a greased or non-stick baking sheet and brush with the beaten egg white. Bake in preheated 425-degree oven about 12 minutes or until golden on top and bottom.

If using a food processor, whirl grated cheese and pepper flakes briefly. Add dry ingredients and mix briefly. Add butter and mix in with pulsating action until coarse crumb texture forms. Add buttermilk and mix until ball forms, then proceed as above.

Yields about 24 small or 16 large biscuits.

Garnishes

Garnishes

*L*et your imagination roam free when it comes to garnishes: A tablespoon of one of the vegetables in the soup, uncooked and cut into a fine dice, adds crunch. In addition to the familiar sour cream, mint, dill, parsley, watercress, chives and lemon garnishes, you might try hardboiled egg rounds, chopped coriander, basil leaves or sprigs of other fresh herbs, chopped nuts, caraway and other seeds, fresh flowers, pretty leaves, citrus twists or flavored croutons. Check the spice rack for a last minute — and very light — dusting of flavor.

Tomato Slush

*S*erve *this tomato garnish on any number of our vegetable-base soups for color and taste contrast or to intensify some of the creamed tomato soups. It looks especially attractive with a creamed cucumber soup.*

1-1/2 cups V-8 juice
3 tablespoons tomato paste
2 tablespoons lemon juice

Mix ingredients together in a bowl, cover and freeze until serving. Keeps almost indefinitely.

Makes approximately 1-1/2 cups.

Toasted Garlic Wafers

12 1/2-inch slices French bread or 6 large slices Italian bread halved crosswise
1/2 cup olive oil
2 garlic cloves put through a garlic press

Combine olive oil and garlic cloves. Brush both sides of bread with oil-garlic mixture, place on baking sheet and bake about 10 minutes in preheated 375-degree oven until golden brown and crisp. Float wafers on top of soup.

Makes 12 wafers.

Sour Cream Toppings

Suitable for soups that do not have a cream base. Mix ingredients together and chill. To serve, top bowls of soup with a tablespoonful.

Topping #1:
1 cup sour cream or Creme Fraiche American Style
2 teaspoons grated lemon peel
1 tablespoon chopped fresh dill

Topping #2:
1 cup sour cream mixed with one of the following:
    1 tablespoon snipped fresh dill or 1 teaspoon dry dillweed
    2 tablespoons minced fresh parsley or cilantro
    1/4 cup minced red or green sweet pepper

Serves 6.

Parsley Toppings

---

*T*hese are particularly tasty with cream soups. Mix together, cover with plastic wrap and refrigerate until serving time. To serve, sprinkle on soup.

Topping #1:
1/4 cup minced fresh parsley
2 teaspoons grated lemon peel
1 small garlic clove, finely minced

Topping #2:
1/4 cup minced fresh parsley
2 teaspoons minced fresh mint
1 small garlic clove, minced fine

Serves 6.

Vegetable Toppings

*T*hese are good garnishes to add extra crunch to creamed soups.Mix together, cover with plastic wrap and refrigerate. Top each serving with a small spoonful.

Topping #1:
1 large tomato, seeded and chopped fine
Tops only of 2 green onions, chopped fine

Topping #2:
1/3 cup seeded cucumber, chopped fine
2 tablespoons celery, chopped fine
2 tablespoons parsley, chopped fine

Serves 6.

Garnish for Curried Soup

*A*lso *good with carrot and squash soups.*

1/3 cup finely chopped walnuts
2 tablespoons shredded coconut
Tops only of 2 green onions, chopped fine

Mix ingredients together, cover with plastic wrap and refrigerate until needed.

Serves 6.

Fresh Flower Garnishes

*R*aid your garden for any of these flowers to float on top of an appropriate soup. The flowers are not only pretty, they have definite flavors as well, ranging from citrus to tart to peppery. Just wash gently with cold water, lay on paper towel and refrigerate until ready to use.

Whole nasturtiums (peppery)
Whole pansies (the miniatures are delightful)
Whole violets (sweet)
Fuschia petals
Marigold petals (citrus)
Chysanthemum petals and leaves (peppery)

Cold Soup Bases

Cold Soup Bases

If you're like most of us, you probably reach for canned chicken broth more often than not when you're making cold soup. But for special occasions — or when you're in the mood — cook up a few quarts of homemade stock or enhance canned broth by adding some extra seasonings. Freeze left over stock in handy 2-cup containers. All stocks and broths should be completely defatted before using.

Cream also gets special treatment in this chapter.

Enhanced Canned Broth

*A*lmost *as good as homemade is this doctored ready-made beef or chicken broth, just the ticket when time is short.*

3 cans beef or chicken broth
1 large carrot, scraped and sliced
1 medium onion, chopped
2 stalks celery, including leaves, chopped
4 peppercorns
2 whole cloves
1/4 cup parsley, minced
1 bay leaf
1/8 teaspoon marjoram

Bring all ingredients to a boil, then simmer, covered, for 25 minutes. Uncover and let stand until cooled. Strain out solids. Refrigerate, covered, for up to 3 days, or freeze.

Makes 4-5 cups.

Homemade Chicken Broth

*T*his broth is both flavorful and practical. By using meaty chicken pieces
as well as the bony wings for extra flavor, you will have meat for a cooked
chicken casserole, a pasta salad or chicken salad.

1 whole chicken breast
1 package chicken thighs, usually 6 pieces
1 package chicken wings, usually 8 pieces
3 quarts cold water, or just enough to cover chicken parts
3 large carrots, scraped and cut in 2-inch pieces
4 stalks celery, with leaves, cut in 2-inch pieces
Extra celery leaves, if available
Handful of parsley sprigs, with stems
1 medium onion, halved and studded with 4 whole cloves
8-10 peppercorns
2 whole bay leaves
2-3 teaspoons salt

Wash chicken parts and put into soup kettle, cover with water and add
remaining ingredients. Over medium heat bring to a gentle boil, partially cover, reduce heat and simmer about 45 minutes. Occasionally
skim off any foam that rises to the surface.

After cooking, pour through a colander. Discard vegetables, though you
might want to save the carrots for that casserole. Line the colander or a
sieve with a double thickness of cheesecloth or strong paper toweling
and pour broth through. Refrigerate broth until fat rises to the top and
congeals. Remove fat and discard.

Pour broth, in 2-cup portions, into freezer containers, allowing room at
the top for expansion. Store in freezer until needed.

Yields about 2 quarts broth.

Homemade Beef Stock

*B*eef bones, browned in the oven, then simmered with vegetables and seasonings, create a rich, intensely flavored broth for both hot and cold soups, as well as gravies and stews. Save and freeze leftover bones and bits of meat to add to the stock.

4 pounds beef bones (marrow, shin, stewing, etc.), cracked by the butcher
Any leftover bones and meat, frozen
5 quarts water
2 cups dry red wine
2 large carrots, chopped
2 cloves garlic, crushed
2 large onions, chopped
3 stalks celery with leaves, chopped
2 turnips, sliced
16-ounce can cooking tomatoes
1 small bunch parsley, coarsely chopped
1 tablespoon salt
6 whole peppercorns
2 whole cloves
2 bay leaves
1 teaspoon thyme

Bake uncooked beef bones in a 350-degree oven until browned. Place in an 8-quart stockpot or other large pot, add the rest of the ingredients, including any leftover cooked bones and meat, and bring to a boil. Lower heat and simmer, covered, 2 to 3 hours or until liquid is reduced by half. Stir occasionally. Let cool, carefully pour through a fine colander to remove solids, cover and refrigerate overnight. Remove all the congealed grease and, if not using immediately, freeze in quart and pint containers for up to 3 months.

Makes about 3 quarts.

Homemade Vegetable Stock

A *handy alternative to chicken or beef broth, especially if there are vegetarians in your family or among your guests. Freeze parings and leftover bits and pieces of vegetables to add to the stock. No need to peel the vegetables — just wash them thoroughly; the solids will be strained out.*

2 cloves garlic, lightly mashed
1 pound carrots, chopped
1 bunch leeks, chopped
5 stalks celery with leaves, chopped
4 onions, chopped
3 small potatoes, quartered
4 turnips, sliced
Any frozen vegetable parings and leftovers
1 stick butter or margarine or 1/3 cup olive oil
6 quarts water
1 small bunch parsley, washed and chopped
28-ounce can tomatoes with juice
10-ounce package frozen spinach, thawed, with juice
10 whole peppercorns
6 whole cloves
3 bay leaves
1 teaspoon each thyme, marjoram and chervil

Melt butter or oil in an 8-quart stockpot or other large pot. Add all vegetables except parsley, tomatoes and spinach and let vegetables "sweat" over low heat, covered, for about 30 minutes. Stir frequently.

Add rest of ingredients, turn up heat to high and bring to a boil. Lower heat and simmer stock, covered, for about 2 hours, or until stock is reduced by half. Stir occasionally. Let cool, then strain through a fine colander to remove solids. If not using immediately, freeze in quart or pint containers for up to 3 months.

Makes about 3 quarts.

Low-Calorie "Cream"

A low-calorie but still tasty substitute for the light or heavy cream called for in the recipes. *Yogurt makes a tangy substitute for sour cream. Use low-fat products for even fewer calories.*

1/2 cup cottage cheese or ricotta
1/2 cup milk

Whirl ingredients in blender until smooth. Add to cooled stock. Do not boil or soup will curdle.

Makes 1 cup.

Creme Fraiche American Style

*T*he thick, slightly sour creme fraiche of Europe can be approximated here by mixing sour cream and heavy cream and letting it stand until thickened. Use as you would either heavy or sour cream. Also good as a garnish.

1/2 cup heavy (whipping) cream
1/2 cup sour cream

Blend the two creams together thoroughly. Mixture will be thin. Let stand at room temperature for several hours or until cream thickens. Cover and refrigerate.

Makes 1 cup.

Easy Cold Soups

Easy Cold Soups

The soups in this chapter rely on ready-made ingredients and are a snap to put together. Keep a few cans of the various ingredients in your freezer or cupboard so you'll always be prepared for spur-of-the-moment entertaining.

Quick New Mexico Avocado Soup with Bacon

*T*he quick and easy preparation of this soup will enable you to spend more time preparing the main course for your menu — or better yet, more time at the pool or on the tennis court.

3 cups chilled, canned chicken broth, all fat removed
2 7-ounce containers frozen avocado dip
1/2 cup water
2 tablespoons lemon juice
1/4 teaspoon garlic powder
1/8 teaspoon hot pepper sauce, or more to taste
1 cup sour cream
6 slices crisply fried bacon, crumbled, for garnish
Chopped sweet red pepper, for garnish (optional)

Add half of all ingredients, except bacon and sweet red pepper, to processor or blender and blend until smooth. Pour into container and repeat with remaining ingredients. Refrigerate for at least 2 hours or until well chilled.

Ladle into colorful earthenware bowls and garnish with crumbled bacon and chopped red pepper.

Serves 6.

Easy Night and Day Consomme

This elegant, easy first course works well with almost any dinner menu; especially nice for warm weather dining is a grilled, marinated leg of lamb with a platter of steamed or raw summer vegetables drizzled with olive oil and sprinkled with fresh herbs.

3 10-1/2-ounce cans beef consomme with gelatin
3 ounces cream cheese, softened
3 tablespoons finely chopped green onion tops
1 tablespoon chopped parsley

At least 2 days before serving, mix 2 cans consomme with softened cream cheese until well blended. Pour into six small glass bowls. Cover with plastic wrap and refrigerate until set.

The day before serving, mix the remaining can of consomme with the chopped onion tops and parsley. Spoon an equal amount of the mixture into each bowl and refrigerate until set.

Serves 6.

Quick Consomme Pick-me-up

*C*ans *of jellied consomme kept in the refrigerator are great to have on hand for spur-of-the-moment entertaining, or for a refreshing low-calorie afternoon treat.*

3 cans jellied consomme, chilled
1 large ripe tomato, diced
1 green pepper, seeded and diced
4-5 scallions, thinly sliced, including some green
6 tablespoons sour cream

Scoop consomme into 6 small glass bowls (or use double old-fashioned glasses) and sprinkle with tomatoes, pepper, onions, and a tablespoon of sour cream.

Serves 6.

Easy Pumpkin Applesauce Soup

A wonderfully easy "off-the-pantry-shelf" soup that is very elegant in flavor. Butterflied leg of lamb and oven-baked, herb-flavored potato wedges go well with this soup.

2 tablespoons butter
1 tablespoon oil
1/2 cup chopped onion
1 cup finely sliced celery
16-ounce can pureed pumpkin
1 cup unsweetened applesauce
4 cups chicken broth
1 teaspoon marjoram, crushed
1 teaspoon salt
1/2 cup sour cream mixed with grated lemon peel, for garnish

In large saucepan saute onion and celery until soft; do not brown. Stir in pumpkin, applesauce, chicken broth and seasonings. Cook, covered, over low heat about 20 minutes. Stir occasionally. Cool and taste for seasoning. Refrigerate several hours or several days. Ladle into bowls and garnish with sour cream.

Serves 6.

Easy Curried Cream of Corn Soup

This is another "off the shelf" easy soup. Oven-baked chicken always tastes right with it; use your favorite recipe.

2 17-ounce cans cream-style corn
2 tablespoons minced onion
1 tablespoon Worcestershire sauce
1/2 teaspoon salt or to taste
1/4 teaspoon white pepper or to taste
2 teaspoons curry powder
1-1/2 cups milk
1 cup light cream
Chopped fresh basil or parsley, for garnish

Blend all ingredients, except garnish, in processor or blender until smooth (do this in two batches). Refrigerate several hours or several days.

Ladle into bowls and garnish with chopped basil or parsley.

Serves 6.

Easy Beet Soup

Plan to serve this gorgeous soup in plain white bowls. Float small white flowers from the garden on top, an especially nice touch for a bridal shower luncheon or other celebration.

1 quart jar ready-made beet soup (borscht), made without beef stock
1-1/2 cups sour cream
Salt and freshly ground pepper to taste

Blend borscht and sour cream in blender until smooth. Chill well. Taste for seasonings and add salt and pepper if necessary.

Serves 6.

Easy-Frosty-Creamy Tomato Soup

A quick, no-cook recipe that transforms canned soup into something special.

2 10-ounce cans cream of tomato soup
1 13-ounce can chicken broth, defatted
1-1/2 cups half and half
1 small onion, coarsely chopped
1 medium cucumber, coarsely chopped
1/4 cup chopped parsley
1 garlic clove, chopped (optional)
1-1/2 teaspoons salt or to taste
1/2 teaspoon paprika
Frozen Tomato Slush, optional, for garnish
Chopped fresh dillweed for garnish

Chill tomato soup and chicken broth. Add soups and half and half to processor or blender. Blend until combined. Add chopped onion, cucumber, parsley, garlic and seasonings, except dillweed, and blend until smooth. Transfer to a serving bowl or tureen and serve with Frozen Tomato Slush (optional garnish) and fresh dillweed.

Serves 6.

Easy Tomato, Lemon and Herb Soup

*T*his is a soup that takes so little preparation time that you can indulge in a more involved second course...or another set of tennis.

1 quart good quality tomato juice
1 1/2 cups boiling water
3 beef bouillon cubes
1 cup finely chopped celery
1 medium onion, minced
1 medium sweet yellow or green pepper, finely chopped
1 garlic clove, pressed
1/4 cup mixed, chopped fresh herbs: parsley, basil, marjoram oregano, tarragon,
    thyme (choose three)
Juice of two lemons
2 ripe tomatoes, coarsely chopped

Dissolve bouillon cubes in boiling water in a large pitcher or bowl. Add tomato juice, celery, onion, green pepper, garlic and choice of herbs. Refrigerate several hours or overnight. Before serving add lemon juice and stir to blend. Ladle into bowls and garnish with chopped tomatoes. Serve with Garlic-Swiss French Bread.

Serves 6.

Easy Blender Vichyssoise

*T*he answer for last-minute entertaining. Chill in the freezer if time is really of the essence.

2 cans frozen condensed cream of potato soup, thawed
2 cups chicken broth
1 cup light cream
Dash of Worcestershire sauce, as necessary
Salt and freshly ground pepper to taste
Sour cream, for garnish
Chopped chives, for garnish

Puree first three ingredients in a blender or food processor until smooth. Taste and add salt and pepper and a dash of Worcestershire if necessary. Chill at least 1 hour. Serve with dollops of sour cream and sprinkles of chopped chives.

Serves 6.

Cold Vegetable Soups

Cold Vegetable Soups

S*ummer's bounty transformed into silken soups that cool and soothe. Today, because so many vegetables are available year-round, you can serve cold soups throughout the year — and there is no reason not to.*

Curried Cream of Asparagus Soup

*B*egin *with this slightly exotic soup, then continue with an entree of grilled lamb kebabs accompanied by currant-studded rice pilaf. Serve a lemon tart for dessert.*

1 tablespoon curry powder
3 shallots, diced
2 tablespoons butter or oil
2 pounds asparagus, sliced, with tips reserved
4 cups chicken broth
Salt and freshly ground pepper to taste
1 cup sour cream (yogurt may be substituted for a tarter taste)
Reserved asparagus tips, for garnish

In a large saucepan, saute the shallots and curry powder in the butter or oil until shallots are soft. Add asparagus, chicken broth and salt and pepper. Simmer mixture about 20 minutes, or until asparagus are quite soft. Let cool slightly, slowly add sour cream, puree in blender or food processor. Taste for seasonings and adjust as necessary. Chill overnight, taste again, and adjust as desired.

Prepare asparagus tips by simmering in lightly salted water until just tender, 3-5 minutes. Drain, rinse under cold water, drain again, and reserve. Serve soup garnished with the asparagus tips.

Serves 6.

Asparagus-Spinach-Chive Soup Lavery

F resh vegetables floating in a flavorful broth could start a homey dinner that includes roast chicken with mashed potatoes and gravy — and hot fudge sundaes for dessert.

12 large spinach leaves, washed well, stacked and sliced thin
18 thin stalks asparagus, sliced on the diagonal into 1-inch pieces
18 fresh chive stalks, sliced into thirds on the diagonal
6 cups chicken broth
1/4 teaspoon chervil
1/4 teaspoon marjoram
Salt and freshly ground pepper to taste
Chopped chives, for garnish

Bring the broth and seasonings to a gentle boil. Add spinach, asparagus and chives and simmer until asparagus is just tender, about 5 minutes. Remove from heat and let cool. Cover and refrigerate. Let come to room temperature before serving. Taste for seasonings and add salt and pepper to taste. Garnish with chopped chives.

Serves 6.

Lillian's Avocado Soup

*T*his is the perfect soup to serve before a meal of chicken salad or poached boneless chicken breasts napped with your favorite tarragon sauce, because you can use the broth in which you've poached the chicken as the base for the cold soup.

2 very ripe avocados, peeled, pitted and chopped
3 cups chicken broth, homemade only
2 tablespoons fresh lemon juice
1/2 teaspoon salt or to taste
1/2 cup sour cream

Add all ingredients to processor or blender and puree until very smooth. Taste for seasoning and adjust. Refrigerate until well chilled but serve same day.

Serves 6.

Blender Avocado Soup

An easy way to use up those avocados that have gotten a little too ripe.

 large soft avocados, peeled, pitted, and chopped
 cups chicken stock, fat removed
 cup light cream
/2 teaspoon ground cumin
 teaspoon salt
uice of 1 lemon
 tablespoons cilantro, chopped, for garnish

Blend all ingredients except cilantro in blender or food processor until creamy and smooth. Chill. Taste again for seasonings and add more salt if necessary. Sprinkle with cilantro.

Serves 6.

Spicy Avocado-Buttermilk Soup

Vegetarian avocado soup. Serve it before your favorite pasta primavera salad. Accompany both with a basket of crunchy breads.

2 very ripe avocados, peeled, pitted and cut into chunks
1/2 cup chopped onions
1 garlic clove, minced
1 teaspoon salt, or to taste
1/2 teaspoon ground cumin
1/2 teaspoon ground coriander
1/2 teaspoon dried pepper flakes
2 cups buttermilk
2 cups low-fat milk
Chopped fresh dillweed, for garnish

Add avocado chunks, chopped onion, garlic. seasonings and 1 cup each of buttermilk and low-fat milk to food processor or blender. Puree until smooth and pour into a container. Stir in remaining buttermilk and low-fat milk and adjust seasoning to taste. Refrigerate at least 2 hours. Ladle into mugs or heavy goblets and sprinkle with dillweed.

Serves 6.

Italian Bean Soup

A *soul-satisfying main course soup. Try it with Crostini or Casseri Toast, crisp green salad and a light red wine.*

3 16-ounce cans white beans, such as Great Northern or cannellini, rinsed and drained
5 cups beef broth
3 tablespoons olive oil
1/2 teaspoon rosemary
1/4 teaspoon oregano
2 stalks celery, chopped fine
2 cloves garlic, minced fine
2 carrots, diced fine
1 large sweet onion, diced fine
1/2 green cabbage, sliced into long shreds
Salt and freshly ground black pepper to taste
4-5 drops hot pepper sauce (optional)

In a large saucepan, bring the beans, broth, celery, carrots, rosemary and oregano to a boil; lower heat and simmer, uncovered, for 20 minutes. Let mixture cool. Remove 1 cup of beans and reserve.

Meanwhile, saute garlic and onion in the olive oil until onion is limp. Add to bean and broth mixture. Puree in batches in a blender or food processor. Add the cabbage and the reserved beans, reheat to a simmer and cook about 10 minutes. Add salt and pepper and optional hot sauce. Chill overnight, taste for seasonings and adjust as necessary.

Serves 6.

Tuscany White Bean Soup with Bacon

This is a variation of the wonderful white bean salads found in Tuscany. Serve as a first course followed by grilled sausages and broiled, herbed tomato halves.

2 1-pound cans white navy beans
4 cups chicken broth
1/2 cup chopped onions
2 garlic cloves, minced
1/2 cup chopped parsley
2 tablespoons torn basil leaves or 2 teaspoons dried
1/2 teaspoon salt or to taste
1/4 teaspoon freshly ground white pepper
6 slices bacon, fried crisp and crumbled

Add all ingredients except bacon to large saucepan. Bring to a gentle boil, reduce heat and simmer, partially covered, about 20 minutes. Cool, then puree in small batches in processor or blender. Refrigerate for several hours or several days.

Serve the soup at almost room temperature. Ladle into white bowls and sprinkle with the crumbled, crisp bacon.

Serves 6.

Cream of Curried Lentil Soup

*Y*ou will probably keep your family or guests guessing just what this soup is; one thing they will all agree on is that it is delicious.

2 cups dried lentils, preferably the red variety
Water for soaking and cooking lentils
1 large carrot, scraped and sliced
3 stalks celery, sliced
1 medium onion, sliced
3 garlic cloves, minced
1 teaspoon each marjoram, crushed, and ground cumin
1 tablespoon curry powder
3 cups beef broth
1 cup water
Salt to taste
1/2 cup sour cream
Chopped parsley, for garnish

Cover lentils with water and soak about 30 minutes. Drain and return to a large saucepan, cover with water, bring to a boil and simmer, covered, about 10 minutes. Drain.

Return lentils to saucepan, stir in all ingredients except sour cream and chopped parsley. Bring to a gentle boil, reduce heat and simmer, partially covered, about 1 hour or until lentils are soft. Cool before adding in batches to processor or blender; puree until smooth. Transfer to a container, stir in sour cream and taste for seasonings. Refrigerate several hours or several days. Soup freezes well; stir thoroughly after thawing or reblend if necessary.

Ladle soup into bowls and serve just slightly cold, sprinkled with chopped parsley.

Serves 6.

Curried Cream of Broccoli Soup

*Y*ou *might like to vary this recipe by substituting cauliflower for the broccoli. Pass a basket of Dan's Beer Biscuits.*

1 tablespoon each butter and oil
1/2 cup chopped onion
4 cups chopped broccoli
3 cups chicken broth
1-1/2 teaspoons curry powder
1/2 teaspoon marjoram, crushed
1/2 cup heavy cream or Low-Calorie "Cream"
1/2 cup milk
1/2 teaspoon salt or to taste
1/4 teaspoon freshly ground pepper
Tomato Slush or chopped cucumber or parsley, for garnish

Saute onions in butter and oil until wilted. Add broccoli and chicken broth, bring to a gentle boil, then simmer, partially covered, about 20 minutes. Remove from heat and stir in curry powder and marjoram. Cool, then stir in cream and milk. Transfer in batches to processor or blender and puree until smooth. Refrigerate several hours or several days. Soup can also be frozen; after thawing, reconstitute in processor or blender.

Ladle into tall goblets or white bowls and garnish with Tomato Slush for optimum effect.

Serves 6.

Cream of Broccoli and Mushroom Soup

This rich soup served with a Chef's Salad would make a substantial lunch. Followed by sliced tenderloin of beef, it becomes an elegant first course.

2 cups coarsely chopped broccoli
3 cups chicken broth
1/2 teaspoon thyme
3 tablespoons butter
1-1/2 cups sliced mushrooms
4 green onions, white part only, sliced
1/2 teaspoon basil, crushed
1/4 cup white wine
1 cup light cream
Salt and freshly ground white pepper, to taste
1/2 cup finely chopped broccoli, for garnish

In large sauce pan combine broccoli, chicken broth and thyme. Bring to a gentle boil, then reduce heat and simmer, covered, about 10 minutes.

Meanwhile, over high heat, saute mushrooms and onions in butter until wilted. Add white wine and basil and cook until almost all liquid has evaporated.

Cool broccoli and chicken broth, then transfer with mushrooms and onions to processor or blender. Puree in small batches until smooth. Stir in cream and taste for salt and pepper. Refrigerate several hours or several days. Soup freezes well; stir thoroughly after thawing.

Garnish with chopped broccoli.

Serves 6.

Cold Cream of Broccoli Soup

*D*id you know that broccoli is one of the most nutritious vegetables? Stock up on health as well as great taste by serving this soup often.

1 large bunch broccoli
1 small onion, chopped
1 small clove garlic, minced
2 tablespoons butter
5 cups chicken broth
Salt and freshly ground pepper to taste
1-1/2 cups heavy cream
18 carrot "matchsticks," for garnish

In a Dutch oven or large saucepan, saute the onion and garlic until translucent; do not brown. Meanwhile, wash broccoli, discard tough end of stem, and break or slice rest into small pieces. Add to onion mixture along with the chicken broth and salt and pepper. Bring to boil, then reduce to simmer and cook until the broccoli is tender. Let cool and puree in batches in blender or food processor. Blend in cream and chill overnight. Taste for seasonings and adjust if necessary. To serve, float 3 carrot matchsticks on each portion.

Serves 6.

Herbed Tomato, Carrot Soup

This very hearty cold soup makes a satisfying lunch accompanied by a crisp salad and hot corn bread.

2 tablespoons butter
2 tablespoons oil
1 pound plus 2 carrots, scraped and shredded
1 cup thinly sliced celery
1 large onion, finely chopped
3 medium tomatoes, quartered
6 peppercorns
1 bay leaf
1 teaspoon basil, crushed
1/2 teaspoon marjoram
1/2 teaspoon thyme
1 slice toast, cubed
1 cup boiling water
3 cups chicken broth
1 cup tomato juice
1 teaspoon seasoned salt

Heat butter and oil in large, heavy saucepan. Add carrots, celery, chopped onion and tomatoes and cook over very low heat, stirring occasionally, just until they turn golden. Add peppercorns, herbs and boiling water. Cover and simmer about 30 minutes. Remove cover and boil down until almost all liquid evaporates. Remove bay leaf and cool before transferring in batches to processor or blender. Puree until almost smooth.

Return to saucepan, add chicken broth, tomato juice and salt. Heat slowly for about 10 minutes. Transfer to a container and refrigerate several hours or several days. Soup also freezes well. Blend thoroughly before serving.

Serves 6.

California Carrot Soup

This would be a refreshing first course followed by chicken with fruit salad and a quick fruit-and-nut bread.

2 tablespoons butter
1 tablespoon oil
1 pound plus 3 carrots, scraped and thinly sliced
1 cup chopped onion
2-1/2 cups water
1 cup fresh orange juice
2 teaspoons grated orange peel
1/2 teaspoon ground cardamom
1/4 teaspoon ground cloves
1 teaspoon salt or more to taste
3-inch piece cinnamon stick
1/2 cup Creme Fraiche American Style or sour cream
Ground cinnamon, for garnish

Heat butter and oil in large saucepan and saute onions and carrots until soft, about 10 minutes. Add water and salt and simmer, covered, about 20 minutes. Cool before pureeing in batches in processor or blender.

Return to saucepan, add orange juice and orange peel, cardamom, cloves and cinnamon stick. Reheat just to a simmer and cook about 10 minutes. Cool slightly, then stir in Creme Fraiche. Remove cinnamon stick and refrigerate several hours or up to 3 days.

Ladle into glass bowls and sprinkle with a dash of cinnamon.

Serves 6.

Carol's Cream of Carrot and Fresh Dill Soup

*F*resh dill is a must for this soup. If you're lucky enough to have fresh garden carrots, the taste will be extra special.

3 carrots, scraped and thinly sliced
1 cup chopped onions
1 tablespoon butter
1 tablespoon oil
3 cups chicken broth, fat removed
1 teaspoon salt
1/2 cup light cream
1/2 cup milk
2 tablespoons finely chopped fresh dill
1/8 to 1/4 teaspoon cayenne pepper

Saute the onions in the butter and oil until wilted. Stir in the carrots, chicken broth and salt. Bring to a slow boil, then simmer, partially covered, 15 minutes. Cool.

Add small batches to a processor or blender and puree until smooth. Transfer to a container, add the cream, milk, dill and cayenne and mix thoroughly.

Refrigerate at least overnight. Soup also freezes well; reblend after thawing. Adjust for seasonings before serving.

Serves 6.

Carrot Vichyssoise

This variation of a favorite classic looks stunning when served in black or other dark individual bowls.

1 pound carrots, scraped and thinly sliced
1 pound potatoes, peeled and thinly sliced
3 leeks, green leaves discarded, split vertically and washed thoroughly, then cut into
    1-inch lengths
2 tablespoons butter
2 tablespoons oil
1 teaspoon thyme, crushed
2 teaspoons dried dillweed
1-1/2 teaspoons salt
1/2 teaspoon white pepper
2 cups chicken stock
1 cup water
1 cup half and half
Fresh dillweed, for garnish

Heat butter and oil in large, heavy saucepan, stir in carrots, potatoes and leeks. Cover and cook over very low heat about 25 minutes or until vegetables are soft. Stir occasionally. Add thyme, dill, salt and pepper and stir in chicken stock and water. Cover, bring to a slow boil and then simmer about 30 minutes. Cool soup before adding in batches to processor or blender. Puree until smooth. Pour into container, add cream and taste for seasoning. Refrigerate for several hours or several days. Soup freezes well.

Ladle into individual serving bowls and garnish with fresh dill.

Serves 6.

Mexican Carrot and Cilantro Soup

Serve this soup in large terra-cotta bowls with crunchy bread and a salad of shredded lettuce, diced tomatoes, avocado and grated cheddar or Monterey Jack cheese for an informal lunch.

2 tablespoons olive oil
4 green onions, chopped
1 pound carrots, scraped and diced
1 large potato, peeled and diced
2 cloves garlic, minced
1/4 cup chopped fresh cilantro (also called coriander or Chinese parsley)
4 cups chicken broth
1 teaspoon coarse salt
1 teaspoon cumin
1/4 teaspoon hot pepper sauce
Picante salsa or taco sauce, for garnish

Saute green onions, carrots, potato and garlic in hot oil for about 10 minutes; do not brown. Add cilantro and cook briefly.

Add chicken broth, salt, cumin and hot pepper sauce, simmer about 20 minutes or just until vegetables are soft. Cool before blending in processor or blender. Puree in small portions, transfer to container and taste for seasoning. Refrigerate several hours or several days.

Ladle into bowls and pass salsa separately.

Serves 6.

Orange-Carrot Soup Hammond

*O*range juice and orange garnish provide the variety for this creamy carrot soup.

8 medium carrots, pared and sliced thin
1 medium onion, chopped
2 cloves garlic, minced
2 cups orange juice
3 cups chicken broth
1/4 teaspoon chervil
Scant 1/8 teaspoon ground nutmeg
Salt and freshly ground pepper to taste
1 cup light cream
6 "twists" of fresh orange peel for garnish

In a 3-quart saucepan, bring carrots, onion, garlic, orange juice, broth, chervil and nutmeg to a boil, reduce heat and simmer, uncovered, for about 20 minutes or until carrots are soft. Let cool, then puree in batches in a blender or food processor until smooth. Blend in cream and add salt and pepper to taste. Cover and chill at least 4 hours. Retaste for seasonings.

Just before serving, remove 6 thin slices of peel from an orange, using a vegetable peeler. Twist one peel over each bowl and let peel float in soup.

Serves 6.

Carrot Soup Winthrop

Nutritious carrots form the basis of any number of tasty cold soups. This one calls for a milk and egg enrichment.

medium carrots, scraped and sliced
medium onion, chopped
cups chicken broth
teaspoon brown sugar
/8 teaspoon pumpkin pie spice (or a combination of ground allspice, ginger,
     cinnamon and nutmeg)
cups milk
egg yolks
Salt and freshly ground pepper to taste
Finely diced carrot, for garnish

Combine carrots, onion, broth, brown sugar, spice and salt and pepper in a 3-quart saucepan and simmer until carrots are tender, about 30 minutes. Let cool slightly, then add milk and egg yolks and cook over very low heat, stirring, until mixture thickens. Do not boil. Puree in batches in a blender or food processor until very smooth. Chill at least 4 hours. Taste for seasonings and correct as necessary. Top each serving with a tablespoon of diced fresh carrot.

Serves 6.

Gingered Carrot Cream

*F*resh *ginger root gives this carrot soup an extra lift.*

1 tablespoon oil
1 medium onion, chopped
2 large cloves garlic, minced
8 large carrots, cut into 2-inch pieces
3 cups chicken broth
2 teaspoons brown sugar
1 tablespoon grated ginger root
1/8 teaspoon cinnamon
Scant 1/8 teaspoon ground nutmeg
1/2 teaspoon curry powder
1 teaspoon salt
1/4 teaspoon white pepper
1 cup light cream
1/4 cup chopped parsley, for garnish

Saute the onions and garlic in the oil until onion is translucent. In a 3-quart pot, simmer the carrots, brown sugar, ginger root, cinnamon, nutmeg, curry powder, salt, pepper, and the onions and garlic in the chicken broth until carrots are tender, about 25 minutes. Puree in batches in the blender or food processor. Add cream and blend well. Chill overnight. Taste for seasonings before serving and correct as necessary. Serve sprinkled with parsley.

Serves 6.

Curried Cauliflower Soup

*E*xotic India is recalled in this spicy puree of cauliflower.

1 head cauliflower, broken into pieces
3 cups chicken stock
2 small cloves garlic, minced
1 medium onion, diced
1 teaspoon ground coriander
1 tablespoon curry powder
5-6 dashes hot pepper sauce
3 ounces plain yogurt
Salt and white pepper to taste
Milk for thinning, if necessary

Cook the cauliflower, chicken stock, garlic, onion, curry powder, coriander, and hot sauce until the cauliflower is tender. Puree in small batches in the blender or food processor. Blend in the yogurt, season with salt and pepper. Chill for several hours or overnight. Before serving, taste for seasoning. Thin with milk if necessary.

Serves 6.

Cauliflower-Caraway Puree

*T*his elegant soup, seasoned with just a whisper of caraway, can begin
dinner in winter or summer.

1 head cauliflower, broken into florets
2 cloves garlic, finely minced
4 cups chicken broth
1/4 teaspoon marjoram
1/4 teaspoon chervil
Scant 1/4 teaspoon caraway seeds
1 cup light cream
Salt and freshly ground pepper to taste
Caraway seeds, for garnish

Simmer cauliflower and garlic in the chicken broth seasoned with the
marjoram, chervil, caraway seeds, and salt and pepper until soft, about 25
minutes. Let cool, then puree in batches in the blender or food processor. Blend in cream. Chill overnight, taste for seasonings and correct as
necessary. Serve lightly sprinkled with caraway seeds.

Serves 6.

Celery, Zucchini and Potato Soup

*S*oothing comfort food. *May be made vegetarian-style, using Homemade Vegetable Stock.*

3 shallots, minced
6 stalks celery, diced
1 tablespoon olive oil
3 large potatoes, sliced
3 medium zucchini, sliced
3 cups chicken broth or vegetable stock
1/4 teaspoon thyme
Scant 1/8 teaspoon rosemary
Salt and freshly ground pepper to taste
1 cup light cream
6 tablespoons celery, finely diced, for garnish

In the oil, saute shallots and celery until somewhat softened, about 10 minutes. Add the potatoes, zucchini, broth, thyme, rosemary, and salt and pepper. Simmer about 25 minutes, until potatoes are soft. Let cool and puree in batches in blender or food processor. Stir in cream. Chill overnight, taste for seasonings and correct as necessary. Serve garnished with diced celery.

Serves 6.

Cold Cream of Celeriac Soup

Celeriac, or celery root, has an intriguingly different flavor. Garden-variety celery may be substituted, but the result is not as special.

1 large celery root, about 1 pound, peeled and diced
2 shallots, minced
1/4 teaspoon thyme
1/4 teaspoon chervil
4 cups chicken stock
1 cup heavy cream
Salt and white pepper to taste
Chopped green onion for garnish

Simmer the celery root and shallots in the chicken broth and herbs until tender, about 25 minutes. Let cool slightly and puree in batches in blender or food processor. To last batch add cream and blend thoroughly. Add to rest of soup. Add salt and pepper to taste. Chill thoroughly, at least overnight. Taste again for seasonings and adjust as necessary. Serve garnished with chopped onion.

Serves 6.

Creamy Celery Soup Foster

*T*he potato gives this soup its creamy consistency; you won't miss the usual cream enrichment. Soup freezes well; reconstitute by whirling the thawed mixture in a blender or food processor.

8 stalks celery, including leaves, chopped
3 medium boiling potatoes, chopped
3 medium onions, chopped
6 cups beef broth
Salt and freshly ground pepper to taste
6 tablespoons fresh celery, minced fine, for garnish

Simmer the celery, onions and potatoes in the beef broth until vegetables are soft, about 25 minutes. Let cool slightly. Whirl in batches in a blender or food processor until smooth. Cover and refrigerate overnight so flavors can blend. Taste for seasonings and add salt and pepper to taste. Stir well if ingredients have separated. Garnish each bowl with some chopped fresh celery.

Serves 6.

El Tamarindo Corn Soup

This soup is a wonderful combination of textures and tastes, smooth and crunchy and cold and hot. Serve with a large bowl of nachos and pass the bottle of hot sauce.

4 cups fresh or thawed frozen corn
4-ounce can chopped green chilies
2 garlic cloves, minced
1 teaspoon oregano
1 teaspoon cumin
2-1/2 cups chicken broth, divided
1-1/2 cups milk
Salt and freshly ground pepper to taste
1 cup peeled, diced tomato, for garnish
1/2 cup chopped green onions, for garnish
1/2 cup chopped cilantro or parsley, for garnish

Add corn, chilies, garlic, oregano, cumin and 1 cup chicken broth to processor or blender and puree. Transfer to a saucepan and add remaining broth, milk and salt and pepper. Bring to a gentle boil, reduce heat and simmer about 10 minutes, stirring occasionally. Transfer to a container and refrigerate several hours or several days.

Ladle soup into terra cotta bowls, if available, and garnish with tomatoes, green onions and cilantro.

Serves 6.

Drew's Corn Chowder

Quickly made with frozen corn kernels. When fresh corn is abundant, slice off kernels to equal 2 heaping cups.

2 10-ounces boxes frozen corn kernels
4 cups chicken broth
1 teaspoon Worcestershire sauce
4 dashes hot pepper sauce
Salt and freshly ground pepper to taste
1 cup light cream
Dillweed, for garnish

In a large saucepan, bring broth to a simmer and add rest of ingredients except cream and garnish. Simmer about 5 minutes, remove from heat and let cool, uncovered. Whirl in batches in a blender or food processor until smooth. Stir in cream. Chill, covered, overnight. Taste for seasonings and adjust as necessary. Garnish each serving with a sprinkle of dillweed.

Serves 6.

Curried Cucumber Soup

*T*his could serve as a starter for a dinner of grilled shish kebab, lentil salad and baklava from the Middle Eastern bakery.

3 cucumbers, peeled, quartered and seeded
3 cups chicken broth
1/4 cup chopped onions
1 teaspoon curry powder
1 teaspoon ground cumin
1/2 teaspoon paprika
1 teaspoon dried dillweed or 1 tablespoon chopped fresh dill
1 cup plain yogurt
1/2 teaspoon salt or to taste

Add cucumbers, chicken broth, onions and seasonings, except salt, to large saucepan. Cover and cook over moderate heat about 10 minutes or until cucumbers are soft. Set aside to cool. Add yogurt to mixture and puree in small amounts in processor or blender. Taste for salt. Refrigerate for several hours or several days.

Serves 6.

Grecian Cucumber Soup

This tastes like a cool Mediterranean breeze feels. Serve with Seasoned Pita Crisps.

2 tablespoons olive oil
1/2 cup chopped onion
2 cloves garlic, minced
3 large cucumbers, peeled, seeded and thickly sliced
3 cups chicken broth
2 tablespoons chopped fresh mint (do not use dried mint)
1 cup plain yogurt
1/2 cup light cream
1 teaspoon salt or to taste
1/2 teaspoon freshly ground pepper
Paper-thin, unpeeled sliced cucumbers, for garnish
Sprigs of fresh mint, for garnish

Saute onion, garlic and cucumbers in hot oil until cucumbers are slightly soft. Add chicken broth and pepper and simmer about 10 minutes. Cool, then puree in small portions, with mint, in processor or blender. Transfer to a container and add yogurt and cream and taste for salt. Refrigerate until well chilled.

Ladle into individual bowls and garnish with sliced cucumbers and mint sprigs.

Serves 6.

Cool-as-a-Cucumber Soup

*C*ucumbers are naturally cool but combined with lime juice, they become positively frigid. Serve with grilled or broiled chicken that has been marinated in lime juice and ground cumin.

3 medium cucumbers, peeled, seeded and coarsely grated
1 cup milk
1 cup sour cream
1 cup plain yogurt
3 tablespoons fresh lime juice
2 teaspoons finely grated lime peel
2 tablespoons finely chopped green onion tops
1 teaspoon tarragon, crushed
1 teaspoon salt
1/2 teaspoon white pepper
Snipped fresh chives, for garnish

Blend all ingredients, except snipped chives, in an attractive serving bowl. Refrigerate overnight or for several days. Ladle into individual bowls and garnish with chives.

Serves 6.

Low-Cal Creamy Cucumber Soup

*U*se our Cream Soup Base to cut down on calories but not on flavor with this refreshing soup. A broiled or poached fish or chicken course, steamed vegetables and gingered melon would complete a low-calorie menu.

1 tablespoon oil
3 medium cucumbers, peeled, seeded and cubed
1 medium onion, chopped
2 tablespoons chopped parsley
2 stalks celery, sliced
3 cups chicken stock
1 cup Low Calorie "Cream"
1 teaspoon Worcestershire sauce
Salt to taste
1/4 teaspoon freshly ground pepper
Chopped red sweet pepper, for garnish

Saute cucumbers, onion, parsley and celery until soft, about 10 minutes. Remove from heat and stir in chicken stock, Low Calorie "Cream", Worcestershire sauce and pepper; taste for salt. Puree in small batches in processor or blender. Refrigerate several hours or several days. Freezes well; may have to be reconstituted after thawing.

Ladle into bowls and garnish with chopped sweet red pepper.

Serves 6.

Mary's Cream of Cucumber Soup

In addition to its refreshing taste is the ease of preparation of this no-cook soup.

3 cups peeled, seeded and coarsely chopped cucumbers
3 cups chicken broth
1/2 cup light cream
1/2 cup sour cream
1/4 cup chopped green onion tops
1/2 cup chopped celery leaves
2 tablespoons chopped parsley
1 clove garlic, sliced
1 teaspoon basil, crushed
Salt to taste
1/4 teaspoon freshly ground pepper
Tomato Slush, for garnish

Puree all ingredients, in small batches, in processor or blender. Taste for salt. Refrigerate several hours or up to a week. Ladle into individual bowls and garnish with Tomato Slush.

Serves 6.

Rosy Cucumber Soup

Serve this tangy and pretty soup with the Double-Wheat Mini Biscuits or your own favorite quick bread or biscuits.

2 large cucumbers, peeled, seeded and diced
16-ounce jar sliced, pickled beets, drained, juice reserved
1/2 cup chopped onions
2 tablespoons chopped parsley
3 cups chicken broth
1 teaspoon sugar
1/4 teaspoon pepper
Salt to taste
1/2 cup sour cream or Creme Fraiche American Style
Chopped green onion tops or chopped chives, for garnish

In two batches, puree cucumbers, beets, onions and parsley in processor or blender, then blend in the chicken broth, seasonings and sour cream; transfer to a container. Taste for seasoning, adding reserved beet juice to taste. Refrigerate several hours or for several days.

Sprinkle with chopped green onion tops or chives before serving.

Serves 6.

Persian Soup Charnizon

A *great start to a company dinner that includes roast leg of lamb seasoned with rosemary and garlic, bulgur wheat pilaf and a salad of green beans, tomatoes, and oregano.*

16 ounces plain yogurt
8 ounces vanilla yogurt
2 large cucumbers, peeled, seeded, and finely diced
1 tablespoon lemon juice
1/2 teaspoon salt
1 tablespoon fresh snipped dill, or 1 teaspoon dried dillweed
1/4 cup chopped walnuts
1/4 cup currants or raisins
2 scallions, chopped fine including some green, for garnish

In a 2-quart bowl, mix together all ingredients except scallions. Chill at least 4 hours, taste for salt and add more if necessary.

Serve in small bowls or cups with the scallions sprinkled on top.

Serves 6.

Minted Cucumber Soup

Popular in Mediterranean climes, this soup translates perfectly to U.S. dinner parties and backyard cookouts.

1/2 teaspoon salt
2 large cucumbers, peeled, seeded and grated
3 cups yogurt
3 small cloves garlic, put through a garlic press
1 teaspoon dillweed or 1 tablespoon fresh snipped dill
3 tablespoons olive oil
2 tablespoons white wine vinegar
10 mint leaves, chopped fine
6 sprigs mint, for garnish

Sprinkle the grated cucumber with the salt and drain in a colander for 20 minutes. Squeeze dry. Blend with the rest of ingredients except garnish. Chill 4 hours or overnight. Taste for seasonings and adjust as necessary. Serve garnished with mint sprigs.

Serves 6.

Green Pea and Watercress Puree

*O*n a hot summer evening a first course of this pale, cool green soup
would soothe the most fevered brow.

2 tablespoons butter
1 tablespoon oil
1 cup sliced green onion, tops only
3 cups frozen peas
1 bunch watercress, tough stems removed, coarsely chopped
3 cups chicken broth, heated
2 teaspoons chervil, crushed
1 teaspoon salt
1 teaspoon sugar
1/2 teaspoon ground white pepper
1/2 cup heavy cream
1/2 cup light cream
Fresh dill, for garnish

In large saucepan saute onion tops in butter and oil until wilted. Add
chicken broth, peas, chervil, salt, sugar and pepper, simmer, partially
covered, about 10 minutes. Add chopped watercress and simmer, uncovered, 5 minutes. Cool soup, then add in batches to processor or blender
and puree until smooth. Stir in cream and refrigerate several hours or
several days. Soup freezes well; reblend after thawing.

Garnish soup with chopped fresh dill before serving.

Serves 6.

Cream of Sugar Snap Pea Soup

*T*he vegetable of the '80s is now refreshing soup.

3 tablespoons butter
2 pounds fresh sugar snap peas, tough strings removed, or 2
    10-ounce packages frozen sugar snap peas
1 bunch green onions, thinly sliced
4 cups chicken broth
1 cup water
2 tablespoons fresh basil, chopped, or 2 teaspoons dried, crushed
12 large leaf lettuce leaves, shredded
1 teaspoon salt or to taste
1/2 teaspoon freshly ground white pepper
1/2 cup sour cream mixed with 2 teaspoons grated lemon peel

Saute sugar snap peas and onions in melted butter until just wilted. Add chicken broth, water and basil, simmer, partially covered, about 20 minutes. Add shredded lettuce and simmer, uncovered, 5 minutes. Cool before adding in batches and pureeing in processor or blender. Transfer to a container and stir in salt and pepper to taste. Stir in sour cream and grated lemon peel mixture. Refrigerate several hours or overnight.

Serves 6.

Minty Double Pea Soup

This soup seems to be just right for serving with a Middle Eastern menu. Pass Herbed Pita Triangles with the soup.

1 bunch green onions, sliced in 1-inch pieces
1/2 cup chicken broth
1/2 pound snow peas, strings removed and cut in half
2 10-ounce packages frozen peas, thawed
4 cups chicken broth
1/4 cup chopped parsley
1/4 cup chopped fresh mint (Do not use dried mint)
1 teaspoon salt, or to taste
1/4 teaspoon freshly ground pepper
Fresh mint sprigs, for garnish

Simmer green onions in 1/2 cup chicken broth until soft, puree in processor or blender; set aside.

Add snow peas, frozen peas and chicken broth to a saucepan and simmer, covered, until peas are tender, about 10 minutes. Add chopped parsley and mint and simmer 5 more minutes. Cool before adding in batches to processor or blender. Puree until smooth, transfer to container and add salt and pepper. Refrigerate several hours or several days.

Garnish each serving with mint sprigs and serve with Herbed Pita Triangles.

Serves 6.

Curried Cream of Pea and Vegetable Soup

A low-calorie curried treat.

10-ounce box frozen peas
2 carrots, scraped and thinly sliced
2 medium potatoes, peeled and thinly sliced
2 stalks celery, thinly sliced
1 medium onion, sliced
2 garlic cloves, minced
4 cups chicken broth, divided
2 teaspoons curry powder
1/2 teaspoon thyme
1/8 teaspoon hot pepper sauce
1 cup heavy cream or Low-Calorie "Cream"
Chopped cilantro or parsley, for garnish

In large saucepan simmer vegetables in 2 cups chicken broth, covered, about 20 minutes or until soft. Cool, then puree in batches in processor or blender. Return to saucepan and add remaining 2 cups broth, curry powder, thyme, salt and hot pepper sauce. Simmer, uncovered, 5 minutes. Transfer to container, cool and stir in cream or Low-Calorie "Cream." Refrigerate several hours or several days. Soup freezes well; reblend after thawing.

Serves 6.

Sweet Pepper Soup

S weet peppers — green, yellow or red, or a mixture — are pureed with broth and topped with olive oil for a first course soup with Italian overtones.

6 medium sweet peppers
5 cups chicken broth
1 medium onion, coarsely chopped
1 teaspoon salt
4 bay leaves
1/2 teaspoon thyme
2 whole cloves
Freshly ground pepper to taste
6 teaspoons extra-virgin olive oil, for garnish

Seed peppers and cut into 1-inch dice. Add peppers, onion and salt to a large saucepan containing the broth. Tie bay leaves, thyme and cloves in a cheesecloth square or bag and add to broth. Bring mixture to a gentle boil, cover and simmer about 30 minutes. Let cool, uncovered. Discard cheesecloth with spices. Puree pepper mixture in batches in a blender or food processor. Taste for salt and pepper and adjust as necessary.

Return puree to saucepan and simmer, uncovered, until slightly thickened. Cool, cover and refrigerate. Reconstitute in blender before serving. At serving time, spoon soup into 6 small bowls and float a teaspoon of olive oil on top of each serving.

Serves 6.

Molly's Favorite Pepper Soup

*S*weet *red peppers add a rosy glow to this simple soup.*

2 tablespoons olive oil
1 large onion, chopped
2 cloves garlic, minced
6 large red peppers, seeded and diced
3 cups beef broth
1/8 teaspoon thyme
Salt and freshly ground pepper to taste
1 cup heavy cream
Chopped parsley, for garnish

Saute the onion and garlic in the oil until soft. Add the peppers, broth, thyme and salt and pepper to taste. Simmer about 25 minutes or until peppers are soft. Let cool. Whirl in batches in a blender or food processor until smooth. Stir in cream, cover and refrigerate at least overnight. Stir well before serving. Serve sprinkled with chopped parsley.

Serves 6.

Puree of Root Vegetables

A melange of root vegetables, cooked long and slow then pureed with cream, is a soothing way to begin a meal on a rare warm day in late fall.

3 tablespoons butter
2 large onions, diced
1 bunch leeks, cleaned well and sliced thin with some green
1 clove garlic, minced
4 large potatoes, diced
2 large turnips, diced
4 large carrots, sliced
5 cups chicken broth
1 bay leaf
1/2 teaspoon marjoram
Salt and freshly ground pepper to taste
1 cup heavy cream
Sour cream, for garnish
Snipped chives, for garnish

In a large saucepan, saute the onions, garlic, and leeks in the butter until lightly browned. Add the other vegetables, chicken broth, bay leaf, marjoram and salt and pepper. Bring to boil, then reduce to a slow simmer. Cook until vegetables are very soft, about 30 minutes. Remove bay leaf, then puree mixture in a blender or food processor until smooth. Blend in cream. Chill overnight. Taste for seasonings and adjust as necessary. Garnish with sour cream and chives.

Serves 6.

Watercress Soup with Potato

*P*eppery watercress makes an appetite-stimulating first course. You might follow it with a hearty entree of Italian sausages baked with various root vegetables seasoned with olive oil, rosemary and lots of salt and pepper.

2 tablespoons olive oil
2 large onions, chopped
3 garlic cloves, minced
6 cups chicken broth
1 large potato, sliced
2 bunches watercress, chopped, with tough stems removed
1 cup light cream
Salt and freshly ground pepper to taste
Juice of 1 lemon
Ground nutmeg, for garnish

In a Dutch oven, saute onions and garlic in the olive oil until onion is translucent. Add the broth and potatoes and simmer until potatoes are soft, about 25 minutes. Add watercress and simmer 5 more minutes. Let cool, then puree in batches in a blender or food processor. Add cream and salt and pepper to taste. Cover and chill overnight. Stir in lemon juice and more salt and pepper as necessary. Serve sprinkled very lightly with nutmeg.

Serves 6.

Low-Cal Vichyssoise

A diet or dietary restrictions are no reason to pass up this sensible version of everyone's favorite.

2 tablespoons oil
4 leeks, white part only, thoroughly washed and sliced
3 cups chicken broth
2 large white potatoes, not baking variety, peeled and thinly sliced
1 garlic clove, minced
1-1/2 cups Low-Calorie "Cream"
1/2 teaspoon salt or to taste
1/4 teaspoon freshly ground white pepper
Finely chopped green onion tops mixed with 1 teaspoon grated lemon peel, for garnish

In large saucepan cook leeks in oil until wilted. Add chicken stock, potatoes and garlic. Bring to a gentle boil, cover and simmer about 20 minutes or until potatoes are soft. Cool before transferring in small batches to processor or blender. Reserve part of the broth until after the Low-Calorie "Cream" is added, then thin soup accordingly. Taste for salt and pepper and adjust. Refrigerate several hours or several days. Soup freezes well; after thawing stir thoroughly or reconstitute in processor or blender.

Ladle into bowls and garnish with green onion and lemon mixture.

Serves 6.

Sweet Potato and Coconut Soup

This soup could be the first course for a Hawaiian-style dinner. Follow with a hot or cold spicy cranberry-glazed pork roast and your favorite rice salad.

3 cups chicken broth
1 medium onion, quartered
1 large stalk celery, with leaves, cut into pieces
2 allspice berries
2 bay leaves
6 whole cloves
1 teaspoon salt
6 peppercorns
1-1/2 pound sweet potatoes, or yams, peeled and cubed
2 cups frozen coconut milk, thawed
1/4 cup chopped cilantro or parsley, for garnish
1/4 cup toasted coconut, for garnish

Add chicken broth, onion, celery and seasonings to medium saucepan and simmer, partially covered, for 20 minutes. Strain broth into large saucepan and add cubed sweet potatoes. Simmer, covered, 20-30 minutes or until potatoes are soft. Cool before pureeing in small batches in processor or blender. Transfer to a container and stir in coconut milk. Refrigerate for several hours or up to 4 days before serving.

Ladle into small bowls and garnish with chopped cilantro and toasted coconut.

Serves 6.

Sunny Curried Sweet Potato Soup

*S*erve *this subtly spicy soup in large mugs, then continue with honey-glazed grilled chicken and roasted-in-the husk corn for an easy summer dinner.*

2 pounds sweet potatoes, cooked in their skins, then peeled and mashed
2 tablespoons butter
1/2 cup finely chopped onions
2 teaspoons curry powder
1 teaspon coriander
1/2 teaspoon ground allspice
4 cups chicken broth
1/2 teaspoon salt or to taste
1 cup light cream
Chopped fresh parsley, for garnish

In a large saucepan saute the onions until wilted and golden. Stir in the curry powder, coriander and allspice. Add the mashed sweet potatoes, then stir in the chicken broth and salt. Cook about 20 minutes. Cool, then refrigerate several hours or up to one week. Soup freezes well.

Whisk or stir thoroughly before serving. Sprinkle each serving with chopped parsley.

Serves 6.

Cream of Sorrel Soup

Sorrel, also known as sour grass, is often found in Eastern European cuisines. Try this recipe when you come across fresh sorrel in the supermarket.

shallots, chopped
tablespoons olive oil
cups packed sorrel leaves, washed well and cut into long thin strips
cups chicken stock
egg yolks
cup light cream
Salt and freshly ground pepper to taste
Sour cream, for garnish
Chopped chives, for garnish

Saute the shallots in the oil until soft but not brown. Add the sorrel and stir until wilted. (You may need to do this in two batches — just add a little more oil to the second batch.) Add sorrel and shallots to the chicken stock and bring to a boil, then simmer about 10 minutes. Let cool slightly. Whisk together the cream and egg yolks, then add slowly to the cooled soup, whisking constantly. Cook over very low heat, stirring constantly, until soup thickens. Add salt and pepper to taste. Cover and chill overnight. Taste again for seasonings and correct as necessary. Serve with dollops of sour cream and a sprinkling of chopped chives.

Serves 6.

Sunset Squash Soup

*T*he addition of red bell peppers to this somewhat tingly soup will remind
you of the glow of a setting summer sun.

2 tablespoons butter
1 tablespoon oil
1 cup chopped onion
3 cups winter squash, acorn or butternut, peeled and cubed
2 large or 3 medium sweet red peppers, seeded and coarsely chopped
1/2 teaspoon dried red pepper flakes
1/2 teaspoon thyme
1 teaspoon salt
4 cups chicken broth
1 cup light cream
1/2 cup chopped parsley mixed with 1 garlic clove, minced,
     and 1 teaspoon grated lemon peel, for garnish

Saute onions in the hot butter and oil until wilted. Add squash, red
peppers and seasonings, stir together and cook briefly. Add chicken
broth and simmer, partially covered, until squash is soft, about 45 minutes. Cool then transfer in small batches to processor or blender and
puree until smooth. Taste for seasoning. Refrigerate for several hours
or several days. Soup can also be frozen.

Whisk in cream before serving. Ladle into bowls and sprinkle with the
chopped parsley garnish.

Serves 6.

Winter Squash and Apple Soup

*T*hanks to advances in food storage, flavorful winter squashes are available in most supermarkets year round.

3 cups winter squash, butternut or acorn
3 green apples, Greening or Granny Smith
4 cups chicken broth
1/2 cup water
3 slices bread, white or wheat, crusts removed and diced
3/4 cup chopped onion
1 teaspoon salt
1/2 teaspoon freshly ground white pepper
Scant 1/4 teaspoon rosemary
1/2 teaspoon marjoram, crushed
Chopped fresh parsley, for garnish

Halve squash, remove seeds and peel; cut into large cubes. Peel, core
and roughly chop apples. In a large saucepan combine all ingredients
except chopped parsley. Cover saucepan and bring to a boil; remove
cover and simmer about 30 minutes. Cool.

Puree in small batches in processor or blender. Transfer to a container
and refrigerate several hours or several days. Soup can also be frozen;
after thawing, reblend if necessary.

Serves 6.

Lisa's Squash Bisque

A sunny summer soup, its color enhanced by the addition of turmeric. Peanut butter is the mystery ingredient.

2 pounds small yellow squash, trimmed and sliced
1 medium onion, chopped
2 cloves garlic, minced
2 tablespoons butter
4 cups chicken broth
1/2 teaspoon curry powder
1/2 teaspoon turmeric
4 dashes hot pepper sauce
1 teaspoon brown sugar
4 tablespoons smooth peanut butter
1 cup heavy cream
Salt and freshly ground pepper to taste

In a Dutch oven, saute onion and garlic in the butter until limp and golden. Add all other ingredients except peanut butter and cream and bring to boil; reduce heat and simmer soup about 20 minutes, until vegetables are soft. Let cool slightly. Stir in peanut butter. Whirl in batches in a blender or food processor until smooth. Blend in cream, cover and refrigerate at least 4 hours. Taste for seasonings and adjust as necessary.

Serves 6.

Creamed Summer and Winter Squash Soup

This hearty soup would accompany a spicy deli-type pasta salad very nicely.

cups sliced zucchini
cups peeled and cubed acorn or butternut squash
medium potatoes, peeled and cubed
cup chopped onions
cups beef broth
cup water
garlic cloves, minced
/4 cup chopped parsley
teaspoon thyme
teaspoons Worcestershire sauce
alt to taste
cup heavy cream

n large saucepan heat beef broth and water, add vegetables and seasonigs. Cover and simmer about 45 minutes or until vegetables are soft; tir occasionally. Cool, then add to processor or blender and puree until mooth. Taste for seasoning and stir in cream. Refrigerate for several ours or up to one week. Soup also freezes well; whisk or stir thoroughly after thawing.

erves 6.

Crookneck Squash and Pea Soup

*T*hese subtle flavors would complement poached chicken breasts or salmon steaks with tarragon sauce.

2 tablespoons butter
1/2 cup chopped onions
1 garlic clove, minced
3 cups diced crookneck squash
10-ounce box frozen peas, preferably the tiny variety
4 cups chicken broth
1 tablespoon chopped fresh basil or 1 teaspoon dried
1 teaspoon salt
1/2 teaspoon ground white pepper
1 cup plain yogurt
Chopped fresh basil or mint, for garnish

Saute onions and garlic until limp in melted butter. Add squash, peas, chicken broth and seasonings. Simmer, partially covered, about 30 minutes. Cool and add to processor or blender in small batches and puree until smooth. Refrigerate for several hours or up to 4 days.

Stir in yogurt and chopped basil or mint just before serving.

Serves 6.

Mystery Zucchini Soup

*F*or those who might ask, the mystery is the bacon. Serve this with your favorite lasagne and a salad tossed with chickpeas and bits of canned chopped chilies.

3 cups diced zucchini
2 strips bacon, halved
3 cups beef broth
1 medium onion, chopped
2 cloves garlic, minced
1 tablespoon chopped fresh basil or 1-1/2 teaspoons dried
1 teaspoon salt, or to taste
Cheese Croutons, for garnish

Add all ingredients to a saucepan, bring to a gentle boil, then simmer, partially covered, about 20 minutes. Stir occasionally. Cool, then transfer in small batches to processor or blender and puree until almost smooth. The bacon will retain some texture. Refrigerate several hours or several days.

Ladle into small bowls and sprinkle with Cheese Croutons.

Serves 6.

Zucchini and Fresh Basil Soup

*F*resh basil is a must for this soup. You might like to serve this with a
seafood pasta salad and a basket of Quick and Snappy Parsley Bread for a
light supper on a hot summer day.

6 cups thinly sliced, scrubbed zucchini
4 cups chicken broth
1/2 cup torn fresh basil leaves
2 tablespoons fresh lemon juice
1 teaspoon salt or to taste
Sour cream, for garnish

Put zucchini, chicken broth and basil into a saucepan, bring to a gentle
boil, then simmer, uncovered, about 15 minutes. Cool before transferring in batches to a processor or blender; puree until smooth. Taste for
seasoning. Refrigerate several hours or several days.

Stir well before ladling into bowls. Serve with a dollop of sour cream.

Serves 6.

Curried Zucchini Soup

This soup seems to go especially well with lamb or beef shish kebabs cooked on the grill.

2 tablespoons butter
1 tablespoon oil
3 cups scrubbed and thinly sliced zucchini
1/2 cup chopped green onions
2 garlic cloves, minced
2 teaspoons curry powder
1/2 teaspoon ground cumin
3 cups hot chicken broth
1/2 teaspoon oregano, crushed
1 teaspoon salt or to taste
2/3 cup sour cream
Chopped parsley, for garnish

Heat butter and oil in large skillet, add zucchini, onions and garlic, cover and cook over low heat until soft. Stir often. Add curry powder, cumin and oregano and cook 1 to 2 minutes more. Transfer in small batches to processor or blender and puree until smooth. Pour into container and stir in chicken broth and salt. Cool before stirring in sour cream. Refrigerate several hours or several days. Soup also freezes well; after thawing, stir thoroughly before serving.

Ladle into attractive small bowls or mugs and sprinkle with chopped parsley.

Serves 6.

Scallion-Zucchini Soup

*Y*et *another zucchini recipe to try when the garden begins its annual overproduction of the vegetable.*

2 cloves garlic, minced
1 bunch scallions (about 6 or 7), sliced thin and including some green
2-1/2 pounds zucchini, seeded if large, and sliced
3 tablespoons olive oil
3 cups chicken broth
1/8 teaspoon thyme
1/4 teaspoon rosemary
1/4 teaspoon chervil
Salt and freshly ground pepper to taste
Juice of 1 lemon
1-1/2 cups light cream
Lemon peel cut into 18 matchsticks for garnish

Saute the garlic, scallions and zucchini in the olive oil until limp but not brown. Add to a large pot containing the chicken broth and all seasonings except the cream. Simmer about 15 minutes. Let cool, then puree in batches in a blender or food processor. Stir in the cream and chill overnight. Taste again for seasonings and correct as necessary. Serve with 3 pieces of lemon peel per bowl.

Serves 6.

Cream of Pumpkin Soup

A nice way to begin a holiday dinner in the fall or winter.

1 medium onion, diced
2 tablespoons oil or butter
1 16-ounce can pumpkin or approximately 2 cups cooked and mashed fresh pumpkin
3 cups chicken broth
1/4 teaspoon thyme
1/8 teaspoon cinnamon
1/8 teaspoon allspice
Dash of rosemary
Dash of nutmeg
Salt and pepper to taste
1 cup heavy cream
Shelled pumpkin seeds, for garnish

Saute diced onion in the oil in a large saucepan until soft but not brown. Add the pumpkin, chicken broth and seasonings. Simmer over low heat about 15 minutes so flavors can blend. Let cool slightly, then puree in batches in a blender or food processor. Stir in cream. Taste for seasonings. Chill overnight. Serve sprinkled with pumpkin seeds.

Serves 6.

Mushroom-Spinach Puree

*F*rozen *chopped spinach and fresh mushrooms combine to create this earthy soup.*

2 tablespoons olive oil
1 medium onion, chopped
2 cloves garlic, minced
1/2 pound mushrooms, sliced
2 boxes frozen chopped spinach, thawed and squeezed dry
4 cups beef broth
1/8 teaspoon ground nutmeg
1/4 teaspoon marjoram
1/4 teaspoon chervil
Salt and freshly ground pepper to taste
1 cup heavy cream
6 fresh mushrooms, sliced or finely diced, for garnish

In a large saucepan, saute the onion, garlic and mushrooms in the oil until onion is soft but not browned. Add the spinach, beef broth, nutmeg, marjoram, chervil, and salt and pepper. Simmer about 15 minutes, cool and puree in batches in a blender or food processor. Stir in the cream. Chill overnight; taste for seasonings and correct as necessary. Serve garnished with the fresh mushrooms.

Serves 6.

Spinach Cream Barry

This velvety puree of spinach, made easy by the use of frozen chopped spinach, could begin a special dinner of chicken roasted with garlic, lemons and olive oil and surrounded by steamed baby vegetables.

tablespoons butter
shallots, minced
boxes frozen chopped spinach, thawed and squeezed dry
cups chicken broth
/8 teaspoon nutmeg
cup heavy cream
alt and freshly ground pepper to taste
utmeg and sour cream, for garnish

Melt butter in a 3-quart saucepan. Saute shallots until limp but not brown. Add spinach, nutmeg, and salt and pepper; cook about 2 minutes. Add chicken broth, bring to boil, then simmer for 10 minutes. Cool slightly, then puree mixture in blender or food processor. Add cream, blend well, and taste for seasoning. Chill overnight and taste again; adjust seasonings if necessary. Garnish with sour cream and a very light sprinkle of nutmeg.

erves 6.

Creamy Spinach Soup

This is such a healthy soup, how nice that it is also tasty. Cut down on calories and cholesterol by substituting our Low-Calorie "Cream" for the cream.

2 10-ounce packages frozen chopped spinach
1/2 cup water
1/4 teaspoon nutmeg
2 tablespoons butter
1/2 cup chopped onion
3 chicken boullion cubes dissolved in 1-1/2 cups boiling water
1 cup milk
1 cup light cream or 1 cup Low-Calorie "Cream"
1/2 teaspoon thyme
1/4 teaspoon freshly ground pepper
Salt to taste
Sunflower seeds, for garnish

Cook the spinach and the nutmeg in 1/2 cup water about 3-5 minutes. (Time will vary if using a microwave.) Do not drain. Cool.

Meanwhile, saute the chopped onion in the butter. Add to the spinach and puree in processor or blender until smooth. Transfer to a saucepan, add chicken boullion, milk, cream, thyme and pepper. Cook until slightly thickened. Transfer to a container and refrigerate several hours or up to 4 days. Taste for salt before serving.

Ladle into white or clear glass bowls and sprinkle with sunflower seeds.

Serves 6.

Creamed Cold Spinach Soup

This is a very rich soup, so plan your remaining courses accordingly, perhaps grilled meat or poultry, oven-roasted potatoes and a simple salad.

1 pound fresh spinach, thoroughly washed and tough stems removed
2 tablespoons butter
1/2 cup chopped onions
2 teaspoons lemon juice
1 teaspoon grated lemon peel
1/2 teaspoon thyme
4 cups chicken broth, heated
1 cup light cream
4 egg yolks
1 tablespoon finely chopped fresh basil
Salt to taste
1/4 teaspoon freshly ground pepper, or to taste
Herbed Croutons, for garnish

After washing and picking over spinach, stack leaves and slice crosswise as thinly as possible. Heat butter in large skillet over low heat, add onions and saute until soft. Add spinach and cook until wilted; do not burn. Stir in lemon juice, lemon peel and thyme.

While spinach is cooking, mix egg yolks and cream together. Add small amount of broth to cream and mix well. Slowly add cream mixture to remaining hot broth, simmer over low heat, stirring constantly, until broth has thickened. Transfer to a large bowl and stir in spinach mixture, fresh basil, salt to taste and ground pepper. Refrigerate several hours or up to 2 days.

Serve soup lightly chilled and sprinkled with Herbed Croutons.

Serves 6.

Tomato-Vegetable Soup

*T*his is not just another tomato soup.

1 medium onion, chopped
2 carrots, pared and sliced
3 stalks celery, sliced
3 tablespoons oil
3 pounds tomatoes, peeled and coarsely chopped
2 tablespoons tomato paste
5 cups chicken broth
2 tablespoons fresh basil, chopped, or 1-1/2 teaspoons dried
1 teaspoon tarragon
2 bay leaves
1 teaspoon salt or to taste
1/2 teaspoon freshly ground pepper
1 cup sour cream or Creme Fraiche American Style mixed with 2 teaspoons grated lemon
   peel and 1 tablespoon chopped fresh basil, for garnish

In a large saucepan saute the onions, carrots, and celery in the oil until golden and limp. Add the chopped tomatoes, tomato paste, chicken broth, herbs and salt and pepper and slowly bring to a boil. Cover and simmer about 30 minutes. Cool mixture before pureeing in batches in a food processor or blender. Remove bay leaf before pureeing. Refrigerate several hours before serving.

This soup keeps well in the refrigerator for several days and can also be frozen. If the soup separates, reconstitute it in blender or food processor. Pass the sour cream or Creme Fraiche mixture at the table.

Serves 6.

Oriental-Style Tomato Soup

*T*his would be a lovely beginning to a stir-fry dinner or an accompaniment to your favorite oriental pasta salad.

2 tablespoons salad oil
1 cup chopped onions
3 celery stalks, sliced
2 teaspoons minced fresh ginger
3 pounds tomatoes, quartered or 4 16-ounce cans Italian plum tomatoes, drained
5 cups chicken or beef broth
1/2 cup chopped parsley
8 whole star anise*
Salt to taste

In a large saucepan heat the oil and saute until wilted the onions, celery and ginger. Do not brown. Add tomatoes, broth, parsley and star anise. (*Star anise is available in large supermarkets or Oriental grocery stores.) Cover and simmer about 45 minutes, stirring occasionally. Cool, then transfer in batches to processor or blender and blend until smooth. Pour through a fine strainer to remove solids. Taste for seasoning and adjust to taste. Refrigerate several hours. Serve lightly chilled.

Serves 6.

Roaring Twenties Tomato Soup

*Y*ou *might like to serve this soup as a "drink" before dinner with Cheese Straws.*

2 tablespoons salad oil
1/2 cup chopped red onions
1 cup gin
5 pounds very ripe tomatoes, peeled, halved and seeds squeezed out
1 teaspoon marjoram, crushed
1/2 teaspoon basil, crushed
1/2 teaspoon thyme, crushed
2 tablespoons minced parsley
1 teaspoon salt, or to taste
1/2 teaspoon freshly ground pepper
1 cup water

Heat oil in large saucepan, saute onions until wilted. Add gin, heat over low heat and carefully ignite with match. After flames fade, add tomatoes, herbs, salt and pepper and water. Stir to blend and cook, partially covered, about 30 minutes. Pour through a colander. Chill overnight or several days.

Serves 6.

Garlicky Tomato-Yogurt Soup

This is a snap to prepare and neither family nor friends will believe you idn't use fresh tomatoes.

14-ounce cans tomato wedges, juice reserved
cups plain yogurt
garlic cloves, minced
/2 teaspoon seasoned salt
teaspoon marjoram, crushed
tablespoons lemon juice
ye Croutons, for garnish

Add half of tomatoes, yogurt, garlic, seasoning and lemon juice to processor or blender. Puree until smooth. Repeat with remaining ingredients. Thin as desired with reserved juice. Taste for seasoning and adjust. Chill several hours or several days.

Serve in small bowls or chunky goblets. Garnish with Rye Croutons.

Serves 6.

Tomato and Zucchini Soup with Cilantro

*W*hether it's called Chinese parsley, coriander or cilantro, this leafy parsley-like herb has a "fresh air" taste that particularly enhances tomato-based dishes.

2 tablespoons olive oil
4 green onions, finely sliced
3 stalks celery, sliced
2-3 garlic cloves, minced
3 tablespoons minced cilantro, coarse stems removed
2 tablespoons minced parsley, coarse stems removed
1-1/2 teaspoons dried marjoram, crushed
1 bay leaf
1/2 teaspoon thyme
4 pounds ripe tomatoes, roughly chopped
2 tablespoons tomato paste
1/2 teaspoon hot pepper sauce
5 cups beef broth
2 tablespoons olive oil
1 medium zucchini, scrubbed and cut in 1/2-inch dice
1/2 cup chopped fresh cilantro, coarse stems removed

Saute green onions, celery, garlic, cilantro and parsley in oil in large saucepan until wilted and fragrant. Add tomatoes, tomato paste, dried herbs, and pepper sauce. Simmer over low heat about 5 minutes, stir occasionally. Slowly add beef broth and continue cooking at a simmer, partially covered, about 30 minutes or until vegetables are quite soft. Cool before transferring in batches to food processor or blender. Puree until smooth, then refrigerate until serving time. Can be refrigerated for several days or frozen.

Before serving, heat 2 tablespoons olive oil in medium skillet and quickly saute diced zucchini until lightly golden but still crisp. Ladle soup into bowls and sprinkle with zucchini and chopped cilantro.

Serves 6.

Minty Gazpacho

This variation of gazpacho is Greek in character: mint leaves, cumin and turmeric.

2 pounds very ripe tomatoes, halved crosswise and seeds squeezed out
1/2 cup coarsely chopped onion
1/2 cup fresh mint leaves, coarsely chopped
1 tablespoon tomato paste
2 slices white bread, cubed
2 large garlic cloves, minced
3 tablespoons herb vinegar
3 tablespoons olive oil
1/4 teaspoon hot pepper sauce
1 teaspoon ground cumin
1/2 teaspoon turmeric
2 teaspoons salt or to taste
1 medium sweet green pepper, cut in 1/4-inch dice (do not chop in processor)
2 medium cucumbers, peeled, seeded and cut in 1/4-inch dice (do not chop in processor)
2 cups ice water, or more, as desired
Toasted Garlic Wafers, for garnish

Add to processor or blender all ingredients and seasonings except green peppers, cucumbers and ice water. Process until almost pureed. Transfer to serving bowl. Stir in diced sweet pepper and cucumbers and add ice water gradually to desired consistency. Refrigerate several hours or overnight. Float a Toasted Garlic Wafer on top of each serving.

Serves 6.

Tart Tomato and Red Onion Soup

This is a full-bodied, coarse-textured soup that you might like to serve with grilled Italian sausages and crusty Italian bread.

4 large, very ripe tomatoes, quartered
1 large red onion, coarsely chopped
3 tablespoons chopped fresh basil leaves
1-2 garlic cloves, minced
1 teaspoon coarse salt, or to taste
1 teaspoon sugar
2 teaspoons coarse-grained mustard
2 tablespoons lemon juice
2 tablespoons red wine vinegar
1/4 cup olive oil
2 cups good quality tomato juice
1 cup ice water
1 cup sour cream mixed with 2 teaspoons dried dillweed, for garnish

Add tomatoes, red onion, basil leaves, garlic, salt, sugar and mustard to processor or blender and coarsely chop and blend. Transfer to large bowl and whisk in remaining ingredients, except sour cream garnish.

Refrigerate several hours or several days. Taste for seasonings before serving. Spoon a dollop of sour cream in each bowl and pass the rest.

Serves 6.

Tomato-Orange-Lemon Soup

*F*resh tomatoes, oranges and lemons make a refreshing soup to serve before a heavy meal.

1 tablespoon each butter and oil
1/4 cup chopped onion
2 stalks celery
6 large tomatoes, peeled, seeded and coarsely chopped
3 cups chicken broth
1/2 teaspoon dried thyme or 2 teaspoons fresh
1 cup fresh orange juice
1 tablespoon fresh lemon juice
1 teaspoon salt
1/2 teaspoon freshly grated pepper
1/4 cup minced fresh parsley
2 teaspoons grated lemon peel

Melt butter and oil together in a large saucepan, add onion and celery and saute until wilted and golden, about 5 minutes. Add tomatoes, chicken broth and thyme. Simmer, partially covered, about 15 minutes. Cool before blending. Transfer in batches to processor or blender. Blend until smooth.

Transfer to large bowl and stir in remaining ingredients, except minced parsley and lemon peel. Refrigerate several hours or several days. Freezes well.

Taste for seasonings before serving. Mix chopped parsley and grated lemon peel together and sprinkle on top of soup before ladling into individual bowls.

Serves 6.

Soup Salad

This salad is meant to be eaten with a spoon and would be an easy starter for a lunch of deli sandwiches, tall glasses of lemonade and gooey brownies.

2 cups beef broth
4 cups coarsely chopped tomatoes
1 cup shredded cabbage
1 cup diced red or green sweet pepper
1/2 cup finely chopped Bermuda onion
2-3 cloves garlic, pressed
1/2 cup dry white wine
1/4 cup lemon juice
1/4 cup extra-virgin olive oil
1 teaspoon paprika
1/2 teaspoon cumin
1/2 teaspoon ground coriander
1/4 teaspoon hot pepper sauce
Salt to taste

Blend all ingredients in serving bowl, preferably glass, and refrigerate several hours or several days. Taste for seasoning before serving.

Serves 6.

Potato, Tomato, Arugula Soup

A rugula is another of Italy's gifts to the culinary scene. It is similar to a dandelion leaf, has a sharp, peppery flavor and adds great zing to a salad, as well as this snappy soup.

1 tablespoon each butter and oil
1 cup chopped onions
2 cloves garlic, minced
4 cups chicken broth
2 medium potatoes, peeled and diced
4 large very ripe tomatoes, peeled, seeded and coarsely chopped
2 cups packed shredded arugula leaves, tough stems removed
1/4 cup minced parsley
1 cup heavy cream
Salt and freshly ground pepper to taste
Chopped watercress leaves, for garnish

Saute onions and garlic in butter and oil just until wilted; do not brown. Slowly add chicken broth, potatoes and tomatoes. Partially cover and simmer about 20 minutes or until potatoes are soft. Add arugula leaves and simmer uncovered an additional 10 minutes. Cool.

Add in batches to processor or blender and puree until smooth. Transfer to container and stir in parsley, heavy cream, salt and pepper. Refrigerate until well chilled. Can be made several days ahead and can be frozen. Reblend to smooth consistency after freezing.

Garnish with chopped watercress leaves.

Serves 6.

Seaside Tomato, Shrimp Soup

This soup would be a nice luncheon dish served with crusty bread or Cheese Pepper Biscuits. To serve as a first course for a summer dinner menu, continue the seafood theme and serve a grilled or poached salmon entree.

2 tablespoons olive oil
4 green onions, chopped
1 large stalk celery, sliced
2 cloves garlic, minced
3 cups chicken broth
1 cup bottled clam juice
1/2 cup minced parsley, coarse stems removed
1 teaspoon pickling spice, tied in cheesecloth or packed into a teaball
1/2 teaspoon turmeric
1/2 pound raw shrimp, shelled and cut into small pieces
4 pounds tomatoes, peeled, seeded and chopped
1 tablespoon red wine vinegar
Salt to taste
Minced parsley, for garnish

Saute green onion, celery and garlic in oil over low heat until wilted. Slowly add chicken broth and clam juice; stir in parsley and turmeric and add bag with pickling spice. Simmer uncovered about 15 minutes.

Meanwhile, puree tomatoes in processor or blender, reserve. Strain broth through a fine strainer, pressing the solids to extract as much flavor as possible. Return to saucepan and bring to a simmer. Add shrimp and simmer just until shrimp turn opaque, about 2 minutes. Remove from heat, transfer to a container and stir in tomato puree, vinegar and salt to taste. Refrigerate for several hours or up to one day.

Ladle into bowls and sprinkle with minced parsley.

Serves 6.

Tomato and Fresh Tarragon Soup

*O*nly *fresh tarragon should be used in this recipe. A simply prepared entree and dessert of fresh melon or berries would make a tasty but low-calorie meal.*

2 tablespoons extra-virgin olive oil
1/2 cup chopped onions
3 tablespoons fresh tarragon leaves
3 pounds very ripe tomatoes, seeded and coarsely chopped, or
      28-ounce can Italian plum tomatoes, with juice
4 cups chicken stock
2 tablespoons tomato paste (eliminate if using canned tomatoes)
1 bay leaf
1 teaspoon thyme, crushed
1/4 teaspoon hot pepper sauce
Salt to taste

Saute onions in oil until wilted and golden. Add fresh tarragon leaves and bruise slightly with back of wooden spoon. Add tomatoes, chicken broth and tomato paste. Stir to blend. Add remaining ingredients and simmer, partially covered, about 20 minutes. Cool.

Remove bay leaf and blend in batches in processor or blender. Taste for seasoning and refrigerate for several hours until well chilled, or up to a week. Soup also freezes well.

Serves 6.

Cold "Hot" Tomatillo Soup

This would be a good first course for a Mexican theme party or before the kids build their own tostados. Tomatillos look like small green tomatoes but with a paper-thin husk. They are available in large supermarkets or Latin American grocery stores.

2 tablespoons oil
1 medium onion, chopped
2 jalapeno chilies, seeded and finely chopped
1 large clove garlic, minced
2-1/2 pounds tomatillos, husks removed and coarsely chopped
2 tablespoons chopped cilantro or parsley
4 cups chicken broth
Salt to taste
Sour cream mixed with chopped cilantro or parsley, for garnish
Diced avocado tossed in lemon juice, for garnish

Add chopped onion and chilies to hot oil and cook until soft; add minced garlic and heat until fragrant and garlic turns golden. Add tomatillos, chicken broth and chopped cilantro. Cover saucepan, bring to a gentle boil, then reduce heat and simmer about 15 minutes. Cool.

Transfer to processor or blender, in at least two batches, and puree until almost smooth. Refrigerate several hours or up to 3 days.

Ladle into bowls and garnish with sour cream-cilantro mixture and diced avocado.

Serves 6.

Cold Curried Tomato "Soup"

Serve this sensational first course only when tomatoes are at their peak. Try it as an appetizer with drinks before a grilled meat and corn-on-the-cob dinner.

medium to large ripe tomatoes, peeled
medium to large onion
teaspoon salt or to taste
/4 to 1/2 teaspoon freshly ground pepper
cup good mayonnaise
teaspoons curry powder or to taste
teaspoon dried tarragon, crushed

Early in the day or at least 3 hours before serving, peel tomatoes with a swivel-type peeler or plunge into boiling water until skin cracks; remove skin. Chop and put into a large bowl. Grate or finely chop onion and add with salt and pepper to tomatoes. Refrigerate.

In small bowl, mix mayonnaise with curry powder and tarragon. Refrigerate.

To serve, spoon tomato mixture into small bowls and top with a dollop of curried mayonnaise. Have your guests mix the mayonnaise into the soup."

Serves 6.

Vegetable "Cocktail" Soup

*F*or the diet-conscious, omit the cream and add another cup of vegetable juice.

4 cups vegetable juice, such as V-8
1 cup light cream or 1 more cup vegetable juice
3 tablespoons olive oil
1 tablespoon wine vinegar
3 large stalks celery, finely chopped
1 large green pepper, diced
1 bunch scallions, chopped including some green (reserve rest of green for garnish)
1 tablespoon Worcestershire sauce
8 drops hot pepper sauce
1 jigger vodka (or more to taste)
Salt and freshly ground black pepper to taste
1 tomato, diced, for garnish
Scallion tops, slivered, for garnish

Combine all ingredients except garnishes and puree in blender or food processor in batches until very smooth. Chill overnight. Before serving taste again for seasonings and correct as necessary. Serve garnished with diced tomatoes and a few slivers of scallion tops.

Serves 6.

Tomato-Garlic Soup-Salad

A summertime treat when tomatoes are at their peak. Crusty French bread to sop up the juice is an excellent accompaniment.

8 large red ripe tomatoes
3 cloves garlic, minced
4 tablespoons fruity olive oil
Juice of 1 lemon
1/4 cup minced parsley
Salt and freshly ground pepper to taste

Core tomatoes and, using a sharp knife, cut into a 1/2 inch dice; place in serving bowl. In a small bowl, whisk together garlic, oil, lemon juice, parsley, and plenty of salt and pepper. Pour over tomatoes, cover bowl and chill at least one hour so flavors can blend. Stir before serving.

Serves 6.

Fresh Tomato and Orange Soup

A *great picnic soup, carried in an insulated container. Serve in paper* *cups while the hamburgers are grilling.*

6 large ripe tomatoes, peeled, seeded and chopped
1 cup fresh orange juice
Zest from one orange
3 cloves garlic, finely minced
3 tablespoons olive oil
3 tablespoons wine vinegar
1 cucumber, peeled, seeded and diced fine
2 sweet red or green peppers, seeded and diced fine
1 bunch scallions, diced fine with some green
4-5 drops hot pepper sauce
Salt and freshly ground pepper to taste

In a blender or food processor, puree the tomatoes and orange juice. Stir in the other ingredients and chill thoroughly. Taste for salt and pepper and hot sauce and adjust to taste.

Serves 6.

Peppery Tomato Soup

Another fresh tomato soup, this one given a Southwestern tang through the addition of chile peppers.

6 large ripe tomatoes, peeled and chopped
2 small canned green chile peppers, chopped
1 small cucumber, peeled, seeded and chopped
2 tablespoons olive oil
2 tablespoons wine vinegar
1/4 teaspoon marjoram
Juice of 1 lemon
Salt and freshly ground pepper to taste
1 cup sour cream
Chopped cilantro, for garnish

Combine all ingredients except garnish in a food processor or blender and puree until smooth. Cover and chill at least 4 hours. Before serving, taste for salt and pepper and adjust as necessary. Garnish with the chopped cilantro, if desired.

Serves 6.

Tomato-Fennel Soup

Tomato broth, seasoned with fennel seeds, gets crunch and texture from finely diced fresh fennel blended in at the last minute.

28-ounce can Italian plum tomatoes, with juice
2 cups beef broth
1 teaspoon whole fennel seeds
1/2 teaspoon fines herbs (a prepared blend of basil, chervil, chives, marjoram, parsley, savory, and tarragon)
1-1/2 teaspoons salt
Freshly ground black pepper
1 small fennel bulb, pared of tough outer stalks and finely diced
Sour cream, for garnish

In a large uncovered saucepan, simmer the tomatoes, broth, fennel seeds, fines herbs, and salt and pepper for about 30 minutes, until tomatoes are very soft and broth is richly flavored. Let cool, then puree in a blender or food processor. Chill overnight, taste for seasonings and correct as necessary. Just before serving, stir in the fresh fennel. Serve garnished with sour cream.

Serves 6.

Miscellaneous Cold Soups

Miscellaneous Cold Soups

*T*his chapter contains those soups that don't quite fit into any conventional category. Look here if you're searching for something really "different."

Adlerian Cool Garlic Soup

As contributor Bill Adler put it, "You would expect that a head of garlic would make garlic soup strong enough to thwart a herd of vampires, but that's not the case." This delicious soup has a delicate, herbal taste.

1-1/2 quarts water
1 head of garlic, heavy papery shell removed, not inner skin
2 carrots, not peeled, cut into 1-inch lengths
1 large stalk of celery with leaves, cut into 1-inch lengths
1 large onion, quartered
4 sprigs parsley
1 bay leaf
Pinch of crushed sage
Pinch of rosemary
1/2 teaspoon thyme
1-1/2 tablespoons olive oil
Salt and freshly ground pepper to taste

Break head of garlic into cloves. Add to large saucepan with the water and all other ingredients. Bring to a slow boil, then simmer for about 45 minutes. Taste the broth for seasonings after about 30 minutes. Adjust to taste.

Strain the broth into a large container and refrigerate at least overnight. Serve at room temperature with garnish of your choice.

Serves 6.

Lottie's Grapefruit, Vegetable Gazpacho

This soup is practically negative-calories, about 50 per cup. Makes a great pick-me-up during the day.

4 grapefruits, peeled, seeded and quartered
3 tomatoes, halved crosswise and seeds squeezed out
2 cucumbers, peeled, seeded and cut into chunks
3 stalks of celery, including leaves
2 red or green sweet peppers, halved, ribs and seeds removed, then cut into chunks
1/4 cup chopped fresh parsley
1/2 teaspoon salt, or to taste
1/4 teaspoon hot pepper sauce, or to taste
Grapefruit juice, as needed

Puree grapefruit quarters in processor or blender, pour into large bowl or pitcher. Puree tomatoes and cucumbers, add to grapefruit. Puree celery, sweet peppers and parsley, add to bowl or pitcher. Stir pureed pulp together, stir in salt and hot pepper sauce and add grapefruit juice as needed.

Serves 6.

Tarragon Soup Eve

If you have your own herb garden, you probably know that French tarragon is more flavorful than other types. If not, let's hope the supermarket knows.

2 tablespoons fresh tarragon, chopped
6 cups chicken broth
1 1/2 envelopes unflavored gelatin
1/2 cup cold water
2 tablespoons lemon juice
Salt and freshly ground pepper to taste
6 very thin round lemon slices, for garnish

Bring chicken broth to a boil, reduce heat and add tarragon; simmer about 3 minutes. Mix gelatin in water and stir until dissolved. Blend into broth. Let stand, off heat, until cool. Stir in lemon juice and salt and pepper. Cover and refrigerate overnight. Before serving, taste for seasoning and adjust as necessary. Serve the slightly thickened soup in glass bowls and top each serving with a thin round of lemon.

Serves 6.

Creamy Curry-Chutney Soup

*F*or a luncheon menu, serve this soup with a rice and chicken salad, followed by a mixed-melon dessert and crisp cookies.

4 cups chicken broth
1/2 cup finely chopped chutney
1-1/2 teaspoons curry powder, or more to taste
1 egg yolk
1/2 cup heavy cream
2 teaspoons lemon juice
1 teaspoon grated lemon peel
Salt to taste
1 small cucumber, peeled, seeded and diced, for garnish
2 green onions, finely chopped, for garnish

Mix chicken broth, chutney and curry powder together in saucepan and bring to a gentle boil. Meanwhile whisk the egg yolk and cream together. Remove the broth from the heat and slowly whisk in the egg yolk and cream mixture. Return to low heat and simmer until slightly thickened. Add lemon juice and grated lemon peel. Refrigerate for several hours or several days.

Ladle into small bowls and garnish with diced cucumber and chopped green onions.

Serves 6.

Peanut Butter Soup

A sophisticated soup despite its name, full of the tastes of Africa.

5 cups beef broth
1/2 cup smooth peanut butter
8 drops Tabasco-type sauce, or to taste
1/4 teaspoon rosemary
1/4 teaspoon thyme
2 cloves garlic, minced fine
1 small onion, minced fine
1/2 teaspoon ground cumin
1/2 teaspoon curry powder
2 tablespoons olive oil
Salt and freshly ground pepper to taste
1 cup light cream

Saute the garlic, onion, cumin and curry powder in the olive oil over very low heat until onion is soft, about 15 minutes. Add to a large saucepan containing the rest of the ingredients except the cream. Simmer about 30 minutes, let cool, cover and refrigerate overnight. Stir in the cream and adjust seasonings to taste.

Serves 6.

Fresh Herb Soup

A fresh-tasting blend of garden herbs, gathered from your own backyard or the supermarket.

1 small bunch parsley, tough stems removed and chopped
1 small bunch watercress, tough stems removed and chopped
8-10 basil leaves, shredded
2 tablespoons snipped fresh dill
2 tablespoons snipped fresh chives
1 small onion, diced
2 small cloves garlic, minced
1/2 teaspoon chervil
Dash nutmeg
4 cups chicken broth
1 cup heavy cream
3 egg yolks
Salt and freshly ground pepper to taste
18 chive stalks for garnish

In a 3-quart saucepan, simmer the herbs, onions, garlic, chervil and nutmeg in the chicken broth about 10 minutes, or until herbs are soft. Puree in batches in a blender or food processor. Let cool.

Over very low heat, cook the egg yolks and cream, stirring constantly, until slightly thickened. Do not let boil. Blend into herb puree. Add salt and pepper to taste. Chill overnight. Taste again for seasonings and correct as necessary. Garnish with 3 chive stalks per bowl.

Serves 6.

Zingy Vegetable-Cranberry Soup

A perfect first course for a dinner of Turkey Tonnato, which is a variation of the summer classic, Veal Tonnato.

2 tablespoons butter
1 tablespoon oil
1/2 cup chopped onions
1/2 cup thinly sliced carrots
1/2 cup thinly sliced celery
2 cups chicken broth
1 3-inch cinnamon stick
1/2 teaspoon ground cloves
1/2 teaspoon dried red pepper flakes
1/2 teaspoon salt
1 12-ounce bag fresh or frozen cranberries, rinsed and picked over
2 cups apple juice, or more to thin soup
1 cup sour cream mixed with 2 teaspoons sugar and 1/4 teaspoon cinnamon, for garnish

Saute onions, carrots and celery in butter and oil until soft. Add chicken broth, cinnamon stick, cloves, red pepper flakes and salt, bring to a gentle boil and simmer, covered, 10 minutes.

Add cranberries to the saucepan and simmer until berries start to pop. Cool, remove cinnamon stick, then puree soup in batches in processor or blender. Pour into container and stir in apple juice. Refrigerate several hours or several days. Soup can also be frozen.

Stir soup thoroughly before ladling into earthenware bowls and garnish with dollops of sour cream or pass cream separately.

Serves 6.

Cold Fruit and Dessert Soups

Cold Fruit and Dessert Soups

*F*ruit and cream, perhaps spiked with wine or champagne, is a refreshing— and different — way to end a meal. Even more unusual is a fruit soup for a first course, or even a main one. This chapter contains fruit-based soups, some definitely desserts and others that can be served anytime. Let your spirit of adventure be your guide.

Champagne-Berry Soup

*B*erries *and cream with the extra fillip of champagne. Pass lacy cookies and serve the rest of the champagne to sip for a cool, light dessert.*

3 cups strawberries, hulled and washed
6 strawberries with stems for garnish
1/2 cup sugar
2 cups heavy cream
1 cup not-too-dry champagne

Puree the berries and sugar in a blender or food processor. Blend well with the cream. Chill and taste again for sugar. Just before serving, stir in the champagne. Serve the soup in glass bowls or stemmed glasses, and garnish with the whole berries.

Serves 6.

Peach-Blueberry Soup

A sprightly sugar syrup is combined with peaches and blueberries for a cool summer dessert. Serve with almond cookies.

6 large ripe peaches, peeled, seeded and cut into thin slices
1 pint box blueberries, washed and picked over
2 cups water
3/4 cup sugar
Zest of 2 lemons
Zest of 1 orange
1/2 teaspoon almond extract

In a 1-quart saucepan, simmer the water, sugar, zest and almond extract, uncovered, about 20 minutes. Let cool, then add peaches and blueberries. Refrigerate and chill at least 4 hours or preferably overnight.

The almond cookies may be crushed and spread over the top of the fruit soup.

Serves 6.

Pear Ice Cream Soup

A luscious and refreshing dessert soup. Coconut shortbread cookies make a nice accompaniment.

4 large, ripe pears, peeled, cored and cut into large chunks
Juice of 1 lemon
1/4 cup brown sugar
1/2 cup water
1 teaspoon vanilla extract
1 quart best-quality vanilla ice cream, softened
Mint leaves, for garnish

Bring lemon juice, brown sugar, vanilla and water to a gentle simmer; add pears and simmer-steam about 10 minutes until pears are soft but not mushy. (Add a little more water if necessary to prevent sticking.) Let pears cool in syrup, overnight if possible.

Just before serving, puree the pear mixture and the softened ice cream in a blender or food processor. Pour into dessert bowls and garnish with mint leaves, if desired.

Serves 6.

Raspberry Cream

*T*o pamper yourself and your family on a hot summer day, serve this indulgent soup as a main course, not dessert. Add a bakery loaf of moist walnut-fruit bread, sweet butter and some ripe Brie cheese, and the heat and humidity will seem to disappear. Of course, the soup makes a wonderful dessert, too.

1 quart red raspberries, 6 berries reserved (other berries may be substituted)
1 cup light cream
1 cup heavy cream (2 ounces reserved and whipped for garnish)
1/2 cup sour cream
1/2 cup raspberry-apple juice
2/3 cup exta-fine sugar
Juice of 1 lemon
Reserved berries, whipped cream and 12 small mint leaves, for garnish

Wash and pick over berries; remove any stems. Puree in batches in a blender or food processor along with the sugar, creams and apple-raspberry and lemon juices. Chill thoroughly. To garnish, float a small "island" of whipped cream on the soup and place a berry and two mint leaves on the island.

Serves 6.

Gingered Melon Soup

*M*akes *an interesting first course or dessert, depending on your choice of garnish.*

5 cups honeydew, cantaloupe or other melon, cut into chunks
2 cups water
3/4 cup sugar
2 tablespoons finely chopped fresh ginger root
Seeds of 5 cardamon pods
1 cup heavy cream
6 thin rounds of lime, for garnish
Crushed Italian macaroons, for garnish

In a large saucepan, bring all ingredients except cream and garnishes to a boil, lower heat and simmer 5-10 minutes until melon is soft. Let cool, then puree in batches in a blender or food processor. Blend in cream. Chill overnight. Serve with lime garnish for a first course or topped with crushed macaroons for dessert.

Serves 6.

Mixed Melon Soup

*S*erve this refreshing soup at your next Sunday brunch.

3 cups coarsely chopped, very ripe orange melon: casaba, cranshaw
    or cantaloupe, divided
3 cups coarsely chopped, very ripe honeydew melon, divided
2 cups freshly squeezed orange juice
1/2 cup freshly squeezed lime juice
1-2 tablespoons extra-fine sugar
1 cup Chardonnay or Zinfandel blush wine (either would be nice to serve with brunch)
6-8 strawberries, sliced horizontally

Finely chop enough of both types of melon to yield 1 cup of each; reserve for garnish. Add remaining melon, in batches, to processor or blender; puree with part of orange juice and lime juice. Pour into large glass bowl or pitcher. Dissolve sugar in remaining juice and add to bowl or pitcher. Stir in wine and refrigerate for several hours or overnight.

Serve in tall goblets or cut glass bowls, garnished with sliced strawberries. Or let your guests serve themselves for a more relaxed party.

Serves 6.

Sunrise Melon Soup

---

*W*hy wait until lunch or dinner to enjoy this soup? It's a lovely pick-me-up after tennis, after golf, after cleaning the house.

3 very ripe small cantaloupes, seeded and flesh removed from rind
6-ounce can frozen orange juice concentrate
1/2 cup honey
1/2 teaspoon ground cardamom
1/2 teaspoon cinnamon
1/4 cup peach brandy (optional)
Fresh mint leaves, if available, for garnish

Add cantaloupe chunks to processor or blender and puree. Add remaining ingredients and blend until smooth. Pour into pitcher or container and serve in small bowls, mugs or goblets. Serve well chilled.

Serves 6.

San Juan Melon Soup

A mixed shellfish salad and slices of Garlic-Swiss French Bread preceded by this melon soup would make a satisfying luncheon or light supper after the theater or a movie.

2 large, very ripe cantaloupes, seeded, flesh removed from rind and cubed
2 tablespoons butter
1/2 cup peach preserves
1/4 cup coconut milk
1 cup fresh or reconstituted frozen orange juice
1/2 teaspoon ground allspice
1/4 cup light rum, or more to taste
1 cup heavy cream
Toasted, chopped macadamia nuts, for garnish
Toasted, shredded coconut, for garnish

Saute cubed cantaloupe in butter over low heat until soft. Add peach preserves, coconut milk, orange juice and allspice; cover and simmer until cantaloupe is very soft. Stir in rum and cook, uncovered, 1 or 2 more minutes. Cool, then puree in processor or blender until smooth. Transfer to a clear glass bowl or pitcher and stir in cream. Refrigerate several hours or up to 2 days.

Before serving, stir well and adjust rum to taste. Ladle into small crystal bowls or goblets.

Serves 6.

Peaches and Cream Soup

*L*ate *August and early September are the optimum days for this soup, when the peaches are fat and fairly dripping with juice. Almost as good are frozen peaches; don't bother with the hard rocks the supermarket pawns off as peaches in early spring.*

1-1/2 cups water
1/4 cup sugar
3-inch cinnamon stick
6 whole cloves
6 peppercorns
6 allspice berries or 1/4 teaspoon ground allspice
2 cups Chardonnay wine
3 pounds very ripe peaches, peeled and pitted, or 2 10-ounce packages
    frozen peaches, thawed with juice
1 cup Creme Fraiche American Style or sour cream mixed with 1 heaping
    tablespoon brown sugar

Stir together in saucepan the water, sugar and spices; bring to a gentle boil, then cover and simmer about 30 minutes. Strain out spices and return syrup to saucepan after cooking.

Meanwhile, puree peaches in processor or blender until almost smooth. Cover tightly with plastic wrap and set aside.

Add wine to spiced sugar syrup and simmer, uncovered, about 5 minutes. Cool, then stir in pureed peaches. Refrigerate several hours or up to 2 days.

Ladle into bowls and spoon a generous dollop of Creme Fraiche on top.

Serves 6.

Sherried Apple-Peach Soup

*D*inner on the patio gets off to a promising start with this pretty and tasty summer soup.

6 very ripe fresh peaches, peeled, pitted and sliced
1 cup apple juice
1/4 cup sugar
1/4-inch slice fresh ginger
1/4 cup fresh lemon juice
1 cup sour cream
1/4 cup sweet sherry, or more to taste
Fresh mint leaves, for garnish
Nasturtium blossoms, for garnish

Add peaches, apple juice, sugar and fresh ginger slice to processor or blender and puree until very smooth. Pour into container and stir in lemon juice, sour cream and sherry. Refrigerate several hours or up to 2 days.

Stir well before serving and taste for sherry; ladle into tall goblets or small bowls and add garnish.

Serves 6.

Summer or Winter
Dried Fruit Soup

*J*ust reach into your pantry instead of the fresh fruit bins at the supermarket to cook up this unusual, spicy soup. It's a perfect first course for grilled chicken.

5 cups water
3/4 cup sugar
1 pound mixed dried fruit, prunes removed
2 3-inch cinnamon sticks
6 whole cloves
4 cardamom pods, seeds removed
2 tablespoons lemon juice
1 cup sour cream mixed with 1 heaping tablespoon brown sugar, for garnish

Cook water and sugar in large saucepan, stirring until sugar dissolves. Add dried fruit, spices and lemon juice. Cook partially covered until fruit is soft, about 30 minutes. Remove cinnamon sticks and whole cloves. Cool, then add in batches to processor or blender and puree until almost smooth. Refrigerate several hours or several days.

Serve lightly chilled, garnished with the sour cream and sugar mixture.

Serves 6.

Strawberry Confection Soup

This is definitely the soup to serve for a bridal luncheon or baby shower.

 quart strawberries, rinsed, stemmed and pureed
2 cups water
/3 cup sugar
 cup white Zinfandel wine or other blush wine
 tablespoons raspberry vinegar
 3-inch cinnamon stick
 whole cloves
/2 cup heavy cream, whipped, mixed with 1/2 cup sour cream

 uree strawberries in processor or blender, set aside. Stir together wa-
 er, sugar, wine, vinegar, cinnamon stick and cloves in a large saucepan.
 ring to a gentle boil and cook, uncovered, about 15 minutes. Remove
 innamon stick and cloves, stir in strawberries and simmer, partially cov-
 red, about 15 minutes more; stir frequently. Pour into container and
 efrigerate until cold. Stir in whipped cream mixture.

 erve cool, not cold, in tall whole goblets or small crystal bowls.

 erves 6.

Quick Tart Cherry Soup

*Y*our weekend houseguests might enjoy this for a breakfast beverage
instead of the usual orange juice.

1-pound bag frozen pitted cherries, partially thawed
1 cup berry juice or orange juice, or more as needed
1/2 cup half-and-half
1/2 cup yogurt or sour cream
1/4 teaspoon allspice or cinnamon
Thin slices of orange, halved and slit to rest on edge of soup bowl or mug

In two portions add all ingredients, except orange slices, to processor or
blender and puree until smooth. Add more juice if too thick. Pour into
container and refrigerate overnight or up to 2 days. Garnish with orange
slices.

Serves 6.

Apple and Orange Soup

Apples and oranges are wonderful together in a fruit salad, so why not in a soup? Sip this at brunch before serving your favorite baked egg recipe and a platter of sausage patties, ham and crisp bacon.

2 cups apple juice (or fresh cider if available)
5 eating-variety apples, peeled, cored and coarsely chopped
Juice from 1 lemon
1 teaspoon grated lemon peel
2 teaspoons grated orange peel
1 3-inch cinnamon stick
3 whole cloves
1/2 teaspoon ground cardamom
Sugar to taste
2 cups orange juice
1-1/2 cups heavy cream, divided
1 orange, peeled, sectioned and cut into small dice

In large saucepan combine apple juice, apples, lemon juice, lemon and orange peel, cinnamon stick, cloves and cardamon. Bring to a gentle boil, then cover and simmer over low heat until apples are soft; stir occasionally. Remove cinnamon stick and cloves and cool. Add in batches to processor or blender and puree until smooth. Cover and refrigerate until well chilled. When chilled, stir in orange juice and 1 cup heavy cream. Refrigerate several hours or several days.

Whip remaining heavy cream and fold in diced oranges. Ladle soup into small bowls and spoon a dollop of the whipped cream mixture on top.

Serves 6.

Grandma's Apple and Pear Soup

Some grandmas are the health-food type and would rather make apple and pear soup than apple and pear pie. Serve with an equally healthy pasta salad.

1 pound cooking apples, peeled, cored and cut into chunks
1 pound very ripe pears, peeled, cored and cut into chunks
4 cups apple juice
1 cup water
Juice from 1 orange
Juice from 1 lemon or lime
1/4 cup honey
1/2 teaspoon ground cardamom or 4 cardamom pods, seeds removed
1/4 teaspoon ground cloves
1 cup yogurt mixed with 1 teaspoon each grated orange peel and
    grated lemon peel, for garnish

In a large saucepan combine apples and pears with apple juice, water, orange and lemon juice, honey, cardamom and cloves. Cover and bring to a gentle boil, then simmer about 15 minutes, stirring occasionally. Cool, then remove soft fruit with a slotted spoon to processor or blender, add some of the juice and puree. Pour into a container and stir in remaining juice until soup reaches the consistency you prefer. Taste for sweetness and seasoning and adjust if necessary. Cover and refrigerate several hours or several days.

Serve soup slightly chilled with a dollop of the yogurt mixture.

Serves 6.

Cold Banana Soup

*D*eliciously different. Continue the Caribbean theme with a main course of baked chicken and rice, and serve spicy black beans on the side.

1 large onion, chopped
2 cloves garlic, minced
2 tablespoons oil
1/2 teaspoon ground cumin
1 teaspoon curry powder
1 medium potato, diced
4 cups chicken broth
1 cup light cream
3 large bananas, peeled and cut into pieces
Juice of half a lemon
Salt and freshly ground pepper to taste

Saute onion and garlic in the oil until soft but not brown. Add cumin and curry powder and cook, stirring, about 2 minutes. Add potato and chicken broth, bring to a boil, reduce heat and simmer until potato is very soft. Let cool.

Add bananas and cream. Puree mixture in a blender or food processor until very smooth. Add lemon juice, salt and pepper. Chill overnight; taste for seasonings and adjust as necessary.

Serves 6.

Nina Graybill and Maxine Rapoport are co-authors of THE PASTA SALAD BOOK, COLD SOUPS, and ENJOY! MAKE-AHEAD DINNER PARTY MENUS. They live in Washington, D.C. For many years Ms. Rapoport has pursued a wide range of culinary interests, not the least of which is delighting family and friends with her gift for cooking. Ms. Graybill, a literary lawyer, cooks dinner and writes cookbooks whenever she finds the time.

For Additional Copies of

Cookbooks by Nina Graybill and Maxine Rapoport

Write: Farragut Publishing Company
2033 M Street N.W.
Washington, D.C. 20036

At $10.95 a copy plus shipping charge of $1.05 a copy, send me:

___ copy(ies) of *Enjoy! Make-Ahead Dinner Party Menus*
___ copy(ies) of *Hearty Salads*
___ copy(ies) of *Cold Soups*
___ copy(ies) of *The Pasta Salad Book*

Total ___ books; check enclosed for _____

Name_____

Address_____

City_____State_____Zip_____

Make check or money order payable to Farragut Publishing Company

----

For Additional Copies of

Cookbooks by Nina Graybill and Maxine Rapoport

Write: Farragut Publishing Company
2033 M Street N.W.
Washington, D.C. 20036

At $10.95 a copy plus shipping charge of $1.05 a copy, send me:

___ copy(ies) of *Enjoy! Make-Ahead Dinner Party Menus*
___ copy(ies) of *Hearty Salads*
___ copy(ies) of *Cold Soups*
___ copy(ies) of *The Pasta Salad Book*

Total ___ books; check enclosed for _____

Name_____

Address_____

City_____State_____Zip_____

Make check or money order payable to Farragut Publishing Company